AT CUSTER'S SIDE

Cdr. James Harvey Kidd. Courtesy of the Library of Congress, Washington, D.C.

AT CUSTER'S SIDE

The Civil War Writings of
James Harvey Kidd

EDITED BY
Eric J. Wittenberg

THE KENT STATE UNIVERSITY PRESS
Kent, Ohio, and London

Library of Congress Catalog Card Number 00-062019
ISBN 0-87338-687-6
Manufactured in the United States of America.

06   05   04   03   02   01   5   4   3   2   1

Library of Congress Cataloging-in-Publication Data

Kidd, James Harvey, 1840–1913.
    At Custer's side: the Civil War writings of James Harvey Kidd / edited by Eric J. Wittenberg.
        p.   cm.
    Includes bibliographical references (p.   ) and index.
    ISBN 0-87338-687-6 (alk. paper)
    1. Kidd, James Harvey, 1840–1913. 2. United States. Army. Michigan Cavalry Regiment,
    6th (1862–1865) 3. United States—History—Civil War, 1861–1865—Personal narratives.
    4. Michigan—History—Civil War, 1861–1865—Personal narratives. 5. United States—
    History—Civil War, 1861–1865—Regimental histories. 6. Michigan History—Civil War,
    1861–1865—Regimental histories. 7. United States—History—Civil War, 1861–1865—
    Cavalry operations. 8. Soldiers—Michigan—Biography. 9. Custer, George Armstrong,
    1839–1876. I. Wittenberg, Eric J., 1961– II. Title.

    E514.6 6th .K4 2000
    973.7'474—dc21   00-062019

British Library Cataloging-in-Publication data are available.

THIS BOOK IS RESPECTFULLY DEDICATED to the memories of James Harvey Kidd, George Armstrong Custer, and the men who followed the guidon of the Michigan Cavalry Brigade.

Contents

Fiddlers' Green

Halfway down the trail to Hell,
In a shady meadow green
Are the Souls of all dead troopers camped,
Near a good old-time canteen.
And this eternal resting place
Is known as Fiddlers' Green.

Marching past, straight through to Hell
The Infantry are seen.
Accompanied by the Engineers,
Artillery and Marines,
For none but the shades of Cavalrymen
Dismount at Fiddlers' Green.

Though some go curving down the trail
To seek a warmer scene.
No trooper ever gets to Hell
Ere he's emptied his canteen
And so rides back to drink again
With friends at Fiddlers' Green.

And so when man and horse go down
Beneath a saber keen,
Or in a roaring charge of fierce melee
You stop a bullet clean.
And the hostiles come to get your scalp,
Just empty your canteen,
And put your pistol to your head
And go to Fiddlers' Green.

—Author unknown. Believed to have been written
  in the 1870s, "Fiddlers' Green" was a song sung by
  the troopers of the 6th and 7th Cavalry Regiments.

Foreword

When, in his famous 1884 Memorial Day Address, the future Supreme Court justice Oliver Wendell Holmes proclaimed, "In our youth our hearts were touched with fire," he spoke for a generation of young men who had passed through the pain and glory of the American Civil War. Some, like Holmes, were largely content to internalize the personal legacy of the conflict as they moved on to less sanguine fields of achievement. Others bore the scars and suffering of their ordeal for a lifetime or, encumbered with memories, found the later decades of their lives inevitably diminished by comparison with the recollected glories of their youth.

But there were many veterans of the Civil War who even while embracing the challenges and opportunities of civilian life—establishing profitable careers and immersing themselves in civic and familial responsibilities— sought to preserve the heritage of their wartime service through the power of the spoken and written word. James Harvey Kidd was one of those. His postwar occupations of manufacturer and journalist coexisted with a desire to record the exploits of the 6th Michigan Volunteer Cavalry of Custer's Brigade, in whose ranks Kidd had served with credit and honor, at age twenty-five winning promotion to the rank of brevet brigadier general.

Best known for his 1908 memoir *Personal Recollections of a Cavalryman in Custer's Michigan Cavalry Brigade*, General Kidd rarely passed up an opportunity to speak to veterans organizations on his favorite subject and was called upon to deliver dedicatory addresses at monuments commemorating Custer and the hard-charging "Wolverines." He saw it as a just and sacred duty, worthy of whatever time and effort that entailed, to ensure the Michiganders a "permanent" and "honorable" place in history. In this second volume devoted to the writings of James Kidd—a companion to the previously published wartime correspondence—historian Eric Wittenberg presents a number of Kidd's stirring tributes to his wartime comrades and the charismatic swashbuckler who led them, Gen. George Armstrong Custer.

For James Kidd, service with the Michigan Brigade was truly an exalted remembrance. "It was like a spectacle," he wrote of the great cavalry clash east of Gettysburg, "where the knights, advancing from their respective sides, charge full tilt upon each other in the middle of the field." Although clearly out of sync with our modern-day view of combat, indelibly shaped as it is by the chemical and technological horrors of two world wars, in Kidd's era this chivalric notion of battle was readily accepted by a public who expected military carnage to embody a full measure of "pride, pomp and circumstance." And certainly the jangling spurs and flashing sabers of the horse soldiers seemed the very epitome of military panache.

Kidd's narratives resound with vibrant descriptions of hard-riding, rough campaigning, the beauties of nature, the stern service, and above all the dash and glory of combat of heroic proportions. The student-turned-soldier had a way with words, florid at times, but very much in earnest. And the flamboyant personality of George Custer is omnipresent—a bedizened thread woven through Kidd's martial tapestry.

To say that James Kidd admired General Custer would be an understatement. When he described the golden-haired *sabreur* as "the idol, as well as the ideal of his men," Kidd clearly reflected his own idealism and idolatry. Custer was plainly Kidd's hero. But while glorifying Custer's achievements, Kidd stressed that the General's military prowess incorporated much more than flamboyance and personal bravery. To be sure Custer had "bulldog courage," and seemed "everywhere present" amidst the swirling chaos of battle; but Kidd did not view him as "reckless." Custer was eminently skilled in tactical deployments, his "prescience and intuition" enabling him to size up the situation at a glance, then acting with rapid and decisive initiative. When Kidd noted that "General Custer as a cavalry officer was 'in a class by himself,'" he meant it in the most positive and adulatory sense. Kidd regarded him as nothing less than "the foremost cavalry officer of his time."

Given Kidd's penchant for hero-worship when it came to Custer, it is interesting to see what he has to say about other mounted commanders with whom he served. Kidd describes David McMurtrie Gregg as "a great and modest soldier," perhaps implying a bit of a contrast with that far-from-modest cavalry leader Judson Kilpatrick. Wesley Merritt, while irking Kidd with his off-the-cuff rejection of the latter's postwar narrative of Cedar Creek, was nonetheless gallant on the battlefield, and Kidd praises "his coolness and intrepidity of action." On the negative side of the coin, Kidd dismisses Alfred T. A. Torbert as "a pompous infantry officer but recently assigned to a cavalry command," while division commander James Harrison Wilson "had Kilpatrick's fatuity for getting into scrapes, but lacked his skill in getting out."

Of course Kidd's beau ideal, Custer, failed to get out of the ultimate scrape at Little Bighorn on June 25, 1876. Even in Kidd's lifetime the complex and disputatious events surrounding "Custer's Last Stand" caused some to question the buckskin-clad cavalier's judgment. Today many whose addiction to pop culture outstrips their capacity for historical judgment would deny Custer a place in that metaphorical "Temple of Fame" where Kidd had enshrined him, and relegate him to the sub-basement of military incompetence, if not infamy. While this foreword is not the place to delve into the historical morass of Little Bighorn, suffice it to say that the more thoroughly one researches that battle, the more understandable, and rational Custer's actions become.

When Kidd decided to "touch briefly" on Little Bighorn in his *Historical Sketch of General Custer*, he had no problem assigning full blame for the debacle on Custer's subordinates, Maj. Marcus Reno and Capt. Frederick Benteen. Damning Reno for his "ignominious retreat" from the valley of the Little Bighorn and castigating Benteen for his dilatory response to Custer's order to "Come on, be quick," Kidd is firmly in agreement with many of Custer's modern-day defenders. But in alleging that Custer purposely rode to his death in order to save Reno's companies from destruction, Kidd lapses into romance, if not plain implausibility. And he is quite in error when he states that the trumpeter who bore the last message returned to die with Custer on the hill, since Giovanni Martini (John Martin) lived to 1922. Still it is hard not to admire Kidd's defense of his old commander and the sincerity of his devotion to the glories of the past.

I trust that these pages, suffused with the thundering echoes of hoof-beats and the ringing clash of steel, will serve to keep alive the stirring legacy of those who heeded the call, "Come on, you Wolverines!"

Brian C. Pohanka
Alexandria, Virginia

Introduction and Editorial Notes

James Harvey Kidd, of the 6th Michigan Cavalry, faithfully followed Gen. George Armstrong Custer into battle on many fields during the Civil War. When Custer was promoted to division command in the fall of 1864, Kidd succeeded the Boy General in command of the legendary Michigan Cavalry Brigade, considered by many to be the single finest mounted command in the Union armies. The same age as Custer and witness to most of his greatest exploits, Kidd, understandably, idolized the flamboyant horse soldier.

In 1866, in recognition of his many accomplishments on the field of battle, Kidd received a brevet to brigadier general of volunteers. Born on February 14, 1840, Kidd was a twenty-one-year-old student at the University of Michigan at the outbreak of the Civil War. In 1862 he was commissioned a captain and commanded a company in the newly formed 6th Michigan Cavalry. In the chaotic days following the Battle of Gettysburg, Kidd was severely wounded. Returning to his regiment in the fall after recuperating at his parents' home in Michigan, he was promoted to major and assumed command of the 6th Michigan as its senior officer. By the summer of 1864 he wore the eagles of a full colonel of volunteers.

James H. Kidd was a brave and popular young man who proved himself a leader. His writings document his growth and development from college student to veteran commander, able to inspire men to follow him in battle. He lived a long and productive life after the Civil War, serving as a brigadier general in the Michigan National Guard and publishing two newspapers in his hometown of Ionia, Michigan. As Kidd aged, he took up the task of documenting the accomplishments of Michigan's mounted forces in the Civil War. He left behind a rich historical legacy and many diverse writings, most of which have languished unseen for the better part of a century. Kidd died in 1913, still proudly wearing his insignia of honor as an officer of the Michigan Cavalry Brigade.

Approximately half of the contents of this book were originally intended to be appendixes to my other volume of James H. Kidd's writings, *One of Custer's Wolverines: The Civil War Letters of Bvt. Brig. Gen. James H. Kidd, Sixth Michigan Cavalry* (Kent, Ohio: Kent State University Press, 2000). When I compiled those pieces, I simply restated them verbatim. Upon reflection, however, I realized that there were still many unresolved issues raised in them. As a newspaperman, Kidd was a prolific and talented writer whose words and attitudes reflect the Victorian era in which he lived. While his memoirs, *Personal Recollections of a Cavalryman in Custer's Michigan Cavalry Brigade*, are considered a classic of Civil War literature, Kidd also left behind a number of other important works. Because of this, I decided that a second volume would bring proper attention to his other writings.

These works include Kidd's speeches at the dedication of the Michigan Cavalry Brigade Monument and the handsome equestrian monument to George Custer in Monroe, Michigan. The speech at the dedication of the Custer monument is an especially important work, as it is both a comprehensive sketch of the Boy General's life as well as one of the first documented revisionist views of the tragedy that befell Custer at the Little Big Horn. Kidd places all of the blame for Custer's tragedy on two of his subordinates, Maj. Marcus Reno and Capt. Frederick Benteen.

Two other writings, the speech given on Memorial Day 1885 and the fine description of the mounted charge by the Federal cavalry at the Third Battle of Winchester, have never been reprinted anywhere. Kidd's speech at the dedication of the Custer monument has only been reprinted once, more than twenty years ago and in an extremely limited print run.

This book is intended as a companion volume to both Kidd's memoirs and to the collection of his letters. Taken together they make a significant contribution to our understanding of the trials and tribulations of the horse soldiers who followed Custer's guidon. This volume is not intended to tell the story of Kidd's life; I hope that I have accomplished that task in the volume of letters. These essays are more general in nature, an accounting of the role played by his comrades in the Michigan Cavalry Brigade. I have presented Kidd's exact words in each of the volumes in an effort to tell his story fully, and have made no changes other than occasional punctuation. I hope that I have done justice to Kidd and to the brave young men whose exploits he documented so diligently.

Unlike Kidd's letters, which required considerable narrative material to link them, these essays are independent writings. In those instances where Kidd's own footnotes survive, I have presented them as written, and they appear as footnotes in the text. My annotations appear as endnotes. These writings are presented in the chronological order of the episodes described, and not the order in which he wrote them. The speech at the dedication of the Custer monument, which is a lengthy biographical sketch, is saved for last.

I have not written any connecting narrative or edited these works other than to annotate them in order to make them easier for the reader to understand. I have also added a number of maps that will make it easier to follow Kidd's narratives.

Finally, I include two pertinent items that have long been lost to history. The first is an article that appeared in the *New York Times* in August 1863 and which includes the reports of all four regiments of the Michigan Cavalry Brigade, none of which appear in the *Official Records*. The second is fragment of Custer's lengthy and detailed report of the fighting on the East Cavalry Field, the full text of which is missing and lost to history. This fragment, which appeared in an early biography of Custer, is the only known remaining portion of this report, which, again, does not appear anywhere in the *Official Records*. Any errors in transcription, or in identifying those individuals or incidents discussed in these essays, are solely my own, and I accept responsibility for them as such.

As with every project of this nature, I am deeply indebted to the assistance of many good and generous people. Prof. Gregory J. W. Urwin, of Temple University, who has so carefully documented Custer's contributions to the American Civil War, was the person who first suggested that I compile a second volume of James H. Kidd's writings. I am grateful to him for making the suggestion and also for helping me identify research resources on George Custer's career as an Indian fighter. Greg reviewed this manuscript for me, and I am grateful for his assistance and support. I am also grateful to my friend Brian C. Pohanka for his support. By no means am I an expert on the tragedy that befell Custer and the 7th U.S. Cavalry at the Little Big Horn, but Brian is, having spent much of his adult life studying that critical episode. I relied heavily on his assistance and guidance in annotating the portion of the text of Kidd's speech that dealt with Custer's career as an Indian fighter, including his tragic end. Brian also wrote the foreword to this volume. As always, I greatly appreciate his support and encouragement of my work.

A few others also provided important assistance to this project. My research assistant and friend, Steve L. Zerbe, gathered some of the material that appears in this volume. Susannah B. Warner, of Ann Arbor, Michigan, culled through the rather large collection of Kidd's papers deposited at the Bentley Historical Library at the University of Michigan and was responsible for finding the text of the Memorial Day speech by Kidd that appears in this volume. Dan Wambaugh, of Flint, Michigan, diligently combed through reel after reel of microfilmed issues of both the *Ionia Daily Sentinel* and the *Ionia Weekly Standard*, searching for additional writings by Kidd. Dan found the wonderful account of the charge of the 1st Cavalry Division at the Third Battle of Winchester that graces these pages. Thomas A. Canfield located the *New York Times* article that is the first appendix to this book, and John Heiser, the talented National Park Service historian, assisted in finding some of Kidd's writings for inclusion in this volume. Without his assistance, this volume would not have been possible. Likewise, Blake A. Magner, who also did the maps that appear in the collection of Kidd's letters, prepared the excellent maps that appear in this book.

John T. Hubbell, the director of The Kent State University Press, enthusiastically supported the decision to do the second volume and provided constant encouragement for my efforts. Joanna Hildebrand Craig, editor-in-chief, and Erin Holman, managing editor, once again shepherded me through the labyrinthine publication process, patiently answering my every question. I thank them for their patience and support. We have now done three books together, and I am grateful for the assistance that these good people have lent my work.

Finally, and as always, I owe a great debt of gratitude to my loving wife, best friend, and favorite traveling companion, Susan Skilken Wittenberg, who has always been my rock. Without her unwavering support and tolerance of my endless addiction to the trials and tribulations of Civil War horse soldiers, none of this would have been possible. She is truly the wind beneath my wings. I am, as ever, deeply grateful to her for everything that she has done to make this work happen.

List of Maps

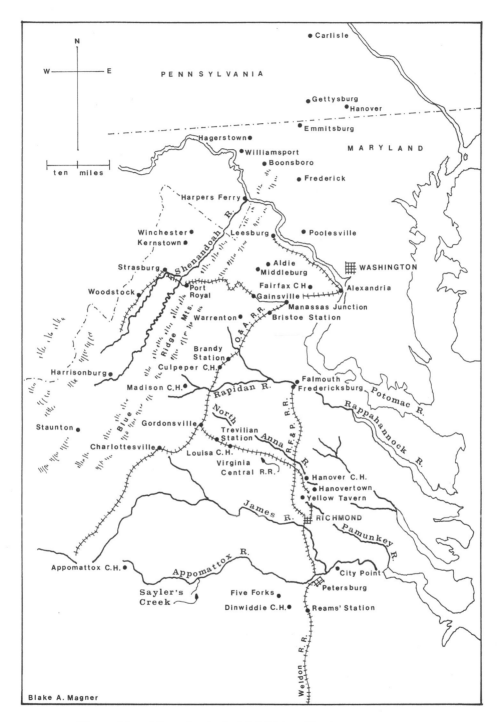

Theater Map of Operations by the 6th Michigan Cavalry

Address of General James H. Kidd, at the Dedication of Michigan Monuments Upon the Battle Field of Gettysburg, June 12, 1889

THE DUTY OF WRITING a sketch of "The Operations of the Michigan Cavalry Brigade in the Gettysburg Campaign," is one which the writer would fain have shirked, had the summons come from a source which he felt at liberty to disobey. It would seem, indeed, that the work had already been done, and well done, so that it will be difficult to add to it anything of positive and permanent value.

It is now nearly five years since the dedication of yonder granite shaft,[*] erected through the liberality of a number of survivors of those who fought here twenty-six years ago, and intended to mark the exact spot where the fierce hand-to-hand saber contest between the hardy Wolverines and the flower of Southern cavaliers took place. On that occasion a distinguished son of the Keystone State,[†] himself a trooper of Gregg's command,[1] delivered a finished and exhaustive oration upon "The Cavalry Fight on the Right Flank of Gettysburg."[2] It was admirably done, evidently a labor of love, and characterized by a spirit of fairness, a moderation, and a judicial tone highly commendable. To peruse its glowing periods is to visit again these scenes. To the writer it is more. It brings back with full force, as if it were but yesterday, the events of that bright July day in 1863, when Gregg and Custer crossed swords with Stuart,[3] Hampton[4] and Fitzhugh Lee;[5]

---

[*]Erected by the survivors of Gregg's (Second) cavalry division and of Custer's (Michigan) brigade.

[†]Colonel Brooke-Rawle, of Philadelphia.

I

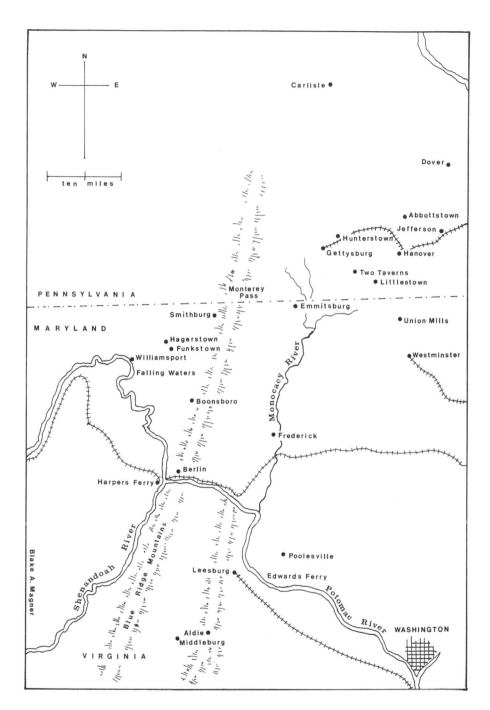

Theater Map of Operations of the Gettysburg Campaign

when the fate of this nation hung suspended by a thread on the plains and heights of Gettysburg. He is once more seated on his horse, in front of his squadron of the Sixth Michigan Cavalry, to the left of Pennington's battery,[6] watching the tumult that is going on below. He hears the rumble and roar, as the earth quakes under the terrible artillery duel on Cemetery Hill[7]; the sputter of the carbines as Alger's[8] dismounted skirmishers drive back the Confederate line; the roar of Pennington's guns, the yells of the troopers as they charge and countercharge. The entire plan is spread out like a picture, and he can see it all again.

A debt of gratitude is hereby acknowledged to Colonel Brooke-Rawle. But, with all due deference to the brilliant orator, it must be said that he speaks with an almost too evident partiality for Pennsylvania and the Second Cavalry Division. His encomiums upon Michigan are perfunctory, and not from the heart. Bright and imperishable chaplets of laurel were gathered here, and our friend would loyally place them upon the brow of his own ideal hero, and not upon that of "Lancelot or another." But there were honors enough to go around, and General Gregg and his command, with their brilliant record, can well afford to render unto Custer and his Michigan Brigade that which is their due. Twice, during the war, the Michigan Cavalry Brigade came opportunely to the relief of the Second Division—once at Gettysburg, and again at Hawes' Shop, May 28, 1864.[9] The mind does not dare consider what might have been the result on either of these occasions had Custer been eliminated as a factor in the contest. If the order which took him to the Hanover Pike on July 3, 1863, was, as Kilpatrick[10] intimates in his report, "a mistake,"[11] it was a most fortunate blunder. This, Colonel Rawle would doubtless be one of the first to admit. There are some controverted [sic] questions concerning the battle which took place on this ground. There are certain differences which, surrounded by the mists of doubt and distance, it is hard to reconcile. The official reports, many of them, are meager, some misleading. The Michigan regiments seem to have been peculiarly unfortunate in this regard. I was unable to find in the War Records office in Washington the official report, written in 1863, of a single one of the commanding officers, covering the operations of the Gettysburg campaign. The maps received from the United States Engineers' office were sent to me with a caution that they must not be regarded as official, since the positions occupied by the different commands have not all, as yet, been definitely determined.

I shall, in the following pages, hew to the line as closely as possible, and endeavor to be as accurate as the accessible data and my ability will permit.

The Michigan Brigade was the outgrowth of the reorganization of the Federal cavalry that followed Lee's invasion of the north and Hooker's consequent movement into Maryland. It consisted, originally, of three regiments—the Fifth, Sixth, and Seventh. They were all organized in 1862, and at the time which we are considering, were, in the language of another, "fresh from pastures green."[‡] The commanding officer was Brigadier General J. T. Copeland, a Michigan man, promoted from the colonelcy of the Fifth.[12] The battalion commanders were, respectively, Colonels Russell A. Alger, George Gray and William D. Mann. The first had seen service in the Second Michigan as captain and major, under Colonels Gordon Granger[13] and P. H. Sheridan[14]; the last in the First Michigan, under Brodhead[15] and Town.[16] Colonel Gray was appointed from civil life, and was having his first experience of "war's rude alarums."

At two o'clock on Thursday morning, June 25, 1863, the brigade, with its division, under Stahel,[17] left its camp in Fairfax county, Virginia, where it had been maintaining a cordon of videttes around the Department of Washington, and the head of column turned toward Edwards' Ferry, on the Potomac river,[18] the Sixth Michigan acting as rear guard. The march was slow, the roads being blocked with wagons, artillery, ambulances, and the other usual impediments of a column of troops in active service. It was long after dark when the rear guard reached the ford. The night was cloudy and there was no moon. The river was nearly, if not quite, a mile wide, the water deep and the current strong. The only guide to the proper course was to follow those in advance; but, as horse succeeded horse, they were gradually borne farther and farther down the stream, away from the ford into deeper water. By the time the Sixth reached the river the water was nearly to the tops of the saddles. Marching thus through the inky darkness, guided mostly by the sound of splashing hoofs in front, there was imminent danger of being swept away, and few, except the most reckless, drew a long breath until the distance had been traversed and our steeds were straining up the steep and slippery bank upon the opposite side.

But, safely across the river, the column did not halt for rest or food, but pushed on into Maryland. To add to the discomfort, a drizzling rain set in. The guide lost his way, and it was two o'clock in the morning when

[‡]Colonel Brooke-Rawle's oration.

the rear guard halted for a brief bivouac in a piece of woods, near Poolesville. Wet, weary, hungry, and chilled to the marrow, as they were, it was enough to dispirit the bravest men. But there was no murmuring, and, at daylight, the march was resumed. That day (26th) we passed the First Army Corps, commanded by the lamented Reynolds,[19] and reached the village of Frederick as the sun was setting. The clouds had cleared away, and a more enchanting vision never met human eye than that which appeared before us as we debouched from the narrow defile up which the road from lower Maryland ran, on the commanding heights that overlooked the valley. The town was in the center of a most charming and fertile country, and around it thousands of acres of golden grain were waving and nodding in the sunlight. The rain of the early morning had left in the atmosphere a mellow haze of vapor which reflected the sun's rays in tints that softly blended with the summer colorings of the landscape. An exclamation of surprise ran along the column as each succeeding trooper, came in sight of this picture of nature's own painting. But, more pleasing still, were the evidences of loyalty which greeted us on every hand as we entered the village. The stars and stripes floated above many buildings, while from porch and window, from old and young, came manifestations of welcome. The men received us with cheers, the women with smiles and waving of handkerchiefs. That night we were permitted to go into camp and enjoy a good rest, in the midst of plenty and among friends.

On Saturday morning (27th), much refreshed, with horses well fed and groomed, and haversacks replenished, the Fifth and Sixth moved on to Emmittsburg, the Seventh having gone through the Catoctin valley by another road.

On Sunday (28th), the Fifth and Sixth, the former leading, moved by way of the Emmittsburg pike to Gettysburg. Thus it was that General R. A. Alger[20] had the honor of leading the first Union troops into the place that was so soon to give its name to one of the great historic and decisive battles of the ages.[§] It was a gala day. The people were out in force, and in their Sunday attire to welcome the troopers in blue. The church bells rang out a joyous peal, and dense masses of beaming faces filled the streets as the narrow column of fours threaded its way through their midst. Lines of men stood on either side with pails of water or apple butter; others held immense platters of bread. Ladies took the slices, covered them with apple

[§]Buford's (First) Division did not arrive until the next day, (29th).

butter, and passed a "sandwich" to each soldier as he passed. At intervals of a few feet the bevies of women and girls, who handed up bouquets and wreaths of flowers. By the time the center of the town was reached, every man had a bunch of flowers in his hand, or a wreath around his neck. Some even had their horses decorated, and the one who did not get a share was a very modest trooper indeed. The people were overjoyed, and received us with an enthusiasm and hospitality born of full hearts.

Turning to the right, the command went into camp a little outside the town, in a field where the horses were up to their knees in clover, and it made the poor famished animals fairly laugh. That night a squadron was sent out about two miles to picket on each diverging road. It was my duty, with a squadron, to guard the Cashtown pike, and a very vivid remembrance is yet retained of the "vigil long" of that July night, during which I did not once leave the saddle, dividing the time between the reserve post and the line of videttes. No enemy appeared, however, and, on Monday (29th) the Michigan regiments returned to Emmittsburg, the First Cavalry Division[21] coming up to take their place in Gettysburg. In this way it came to pass that heroic John Buford,[22] instead of the Fifth and Sixth Michigan, had the honor of meeting the Confederate advance on July 1st.

At Emmittsburg it was learned that many changes had occurred. Among them, Kilpatrick succeeded Stahel, and Custer was in place of Copeland. The Michigan Brigade had been strengthened by adding the First Michigan Cavalry, a veteran regiment that had seen much service in the Shenandoah valley under Banks, and in the second Bull Run campaign with Pope.[23] It was organized in 1861, and went out under Colonel T. F Brodhead, a veteran of the Mexican war, who was brevetted for gallant conduct at Contreras and Churubusco, while serving as lieutenant in the Fifteenth United States Infantry. He was mortally wounded August 30, 1862, at Bull Run.[24] His successor was C. H. Town, who, at the time of which we are speaking, was colonel of the regiment. He also was severely wounded in the same desperate charge wherein Brodhead lost his life. There had also been added to the brigade, Light Battery "M," Second United States Artillery, consisting of six rifled pieces, and commanded by Lieutenant A. C. M. Pennington.

The Third Division was now ordered to concentrate in the vicinity of Littlestown, to head off Stuart, who having made a detour around the rear of the Army of the Potomac, crossed the river below Edwards' Ferry on Sunday night, June 28th, and with three brigades under Hampton, Fitzhugh

Lee and Chambliss,[25] and a train of captured wagons, was moving north-ward, looking for the Army of Northern Virginia, between which and him was Meade's entire army. On Monday night he was in camp between Union Mills and Westminster, on the Emmittsburg, and Baltimore pike, about equi-distant from Emmittsburg and Gettysburg. Kilpatrick at Littlestown was directly across Stuart's path, the direction of the latter's march indi-cating that he, too, was making for Littlestown, which place is on a direct line from Union Mills to Gettysburg.

On the morning of June 30th, Kilpatrick's command, which had been scouting through the entire country east and southeast of Gettysburg, in search of Stuart's raiding column, was badly scattered. A part of it, including the First and Seventh Michigan and Pennington's battery, was at Abbotts-town, a few miles north of Hanover; Farnsworth's brigade at Littlestown, seven miles southwest of Hanover. The Fifth and Sixth Michigan, after an all night's march, also arrived at Littlestown at daylight. The early morning hours were consumed in scouring the country in all directions, and infor-mation soon came in to the effect that Stuart was headed for Hanover. Thither Farnsworth, with the First Brigade,[26] went, leaving Littlestown about 9 or 10 A.M. The portion of the command that was in the vicinity of Abbottstown was also ordered to Hanover. The Fifth and Sixth Michigan were left for a time at Littlestown: Troop "A" of the Sixth, under Captain Thompson,[27] going on a reconnaissance toward Westminster, and Colonel Alger with the Fifth on a separate road in a similar direction.

The Sixth remained in the town until a citizen came running in, about noon, reporting a large force about five miles out toward Hanover. This was Fitzhugh Lee's brigade, and, to understand the situation, it will be neces-sary, briefly, to describe how Stuart was marching. When he turned off the Baltimore pike, some seven miles southeast of Littlestown, he had ten miles, due north, to travel, before reaching Hanover. From Littlestown to Hanover is seven miles, the road running northeasterly, making the third side of a right-angled triangle. Stuart thus had the longer distance to go, and Kilpatrick had no difficulty in reaching Hanover first. Stuart marched with Chambliss leading, Hampton in rear, the trains sandwiched between the two brigades, and Fitzhugh Lee well out on the left flank to protect them.

Farnsworth marched through Hanover, followed by the pack trains of the two regiments that had been left in Littlestown. The head of Stuart's column arrived just in time to strike the rear of Farnsworth, which was thrown into confusion by a charge of the leading Confederate regiment.

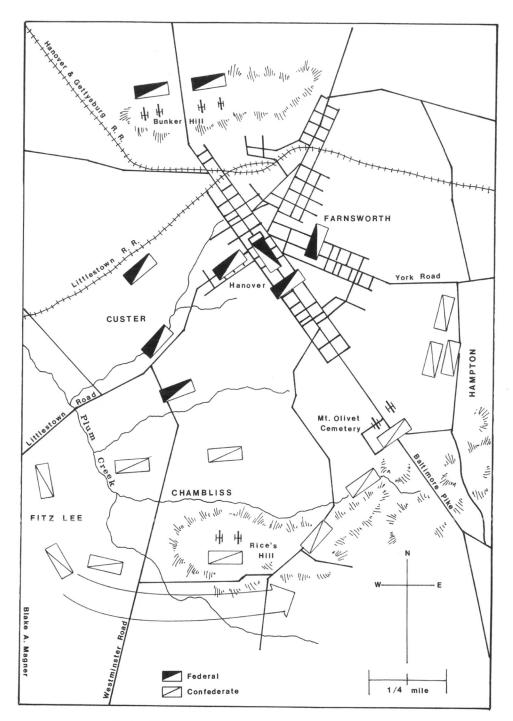

The Battle of Hannover, June 30, 1863

The pack trains were cut off and captured. Farnsworth, however, dashing back from the head of the column, faced the Fifth New York Cavalry to the rear, and by a counter charge, repulsed the North Carolinians, and put a stop to Stuart's further progress for that day.

In the meantime, when the citizen came in with the news of Fitzhugh Lee's appearance, "To horse" was sounded, and Colonel Gray led the Sixth Michigan on the Hanover road towards the point indicated. Several citizens, with shot guns in their hands, were seen going on foot to the flank of the column trying to keep pace with the cavalry, and apparently eager to participate in the expected battle. When within a mile of Hanover, the regiment turned off into a wheat field, and mounting a crest beyond, came upon Fitzhugh Lee's brigade, with a section of artillery in position, which opened upon the head of the regiment (then moving in column of fours), with shell, wounding several men and horses. Lieutenant Potter, of Company "C,"[28] had his horse shot under him. Colonel Gray, seeing that the force in front of him was preparing to charge, and aware that one raw regiment would be no match for a brigade of veteran troops, made a detour to the left, and sought by a rapid movement to unite with the command in Hanover; Major Weber,[29] with one squadron, being entrusted with the important duty of holding the enemy in check while the other companies effected their retreat. Right gallantly was this duty performed. Three charges upon the little band were as often repulsed by the heroic Weber, and, with such determination did he hold to the work, that he was cut off and did not succeed in rejoining the regiment until about 3 o'clock next morning.

Colonel Alger, with the Fifth and Company "A" of the Sixth, also had a smart encounter with the same force, holding his own against much superior numbers, by the use of the Spencer repeating carbines,[30] with which his regiment was armed.

Soon after noon, the entire division united in the village of Hanover, and a vigorous skirmishing was kept up until dark with Stuart's men, who had retired to a commanding position on the hills south of the town.

It was here that the Michigan Brigade first saw Custer, when he appeared mounted on his horse, riding close up to the line of skirmishers, who had been dismounted to fight on foot, giving orders in a tone that was resolute and, to us, reassuring.

Under his skillful hands the four regiments were soon welded together as a coherent unit, acting so like one man that the history of one is apt to be the history of the other, and it is often difficult to draw the line where the credit that is due to one leaves off and that which should be given to another begins.

The result of the day at Hanover was that Stuart was driven still farther away from a junction with Lee. He was obliged to turn to the east, making a wide detour by way of Jefferson and Dover; Kilpatrick meanwhile maintaining his threatening attitude on the inside of the circle which the redoubtable Confederate was traversing, forcing the latter to swing clear around to the north as far as Carlisle, where he received his first reliable information as the whereabouts of Lee. It was the evening of July 2d when he finally reached the main army. The battle had been then going on for two days, and the issue was still in doubt. During that day (2d) both Stuart and Kilpatrick were hastening to rejoin their respective armies, it having been decided that the great battle would be fought out around Gettysburg. Gregg's division had been guarding the right flank of Meade's army on the ground where we now stand, but at nightfall it was withdrawn to a position on the Baltimore turnpike near the reserve artillery. Kilpatrick reached the inside of the Union lines in the vicinity of Gettysburg late in the afternoon, at about the same hour that Hampton, with Stuart's leading brigade, arrived in Hunterstown, a few miles northeast of Gettysburg. It was about 5 o'clock in the afternoon when the Third Division, moving in column of fours, was halted temporarily, awaiting orders to go in, and listening to the artillery firing close in front, when a staff officer of some infantry commander rode rapidly along the flank of the column, crying out as he went, "Little Mac is in command, and we are whipping them."[31] It was a futile attempt to evoke enthusiasm and conjure victory with the magic of McClellan's name. There was scarcely a faint attempt to cheer. There was no longer any potency in a name. Soon thereafter, receiving orders to move out on the road to Abbottstown, Kilpatrick started in that direction, Custer's brigade leading, with the Sixth Michigan in advance. When nearing the village of Hunterstown, on a road flanked by fences, the advance encountered a heavy force of Confederate cavalry in position. A mounted line was formed across the road, while there were dismounted skirmishers behind the fences on either side. The leading squadron of the Sixth, led by Captain H. E. Thompson, boldly charged down the road, and at the same time two squadrons were dismounted and deployed on the ridge to the right, Pennington's battery going into position in their rear. The mounted charge was a most gallant one, but Thompson, encountering an overwhelmingly superior force in front, and exposed to a galling fire on both flanks, as he charged past the Confederates behind the fences, was driven back, but not before he himself had been severely wounded, while his first lieutenant, S. H. Ballard,[32] had his horse shot under him and was left behind, a prisoner. As Thompson's squadron was retiring, the enemy attempted a charge in pursuit, but the dismounted men on the right of the road kept up such a fusillade with their Spencer carbines, aided by the rapid discharges from Pennington's battery, that he was driven back in great confusion.

General Kilpatrick, speaking of this engagement in his official report, says: "I was attacked by Stuart, Hampton, and Fitzhugh Lee, near Hunterstown. After a spirited affair of nearly two hours, the enemy was driven from this point with great loss. The Second Brigade fought most handsomely. It lost, in killed, wounded and missing, thirty-two. The conduct of the Sixth Michigan Cavalry and Pennington's battery is deserving of the highest praise."[33]

On the other hand, General Hampton states that he received information of Kilpatrick's advance upon Hunterstown, and was directed by Stuart to return and meet it. "After some skirmishing, the enemy attempted a charge, which was met in front by the Cobb Legion, and on either flank by the Phillips Legion and the Second South Carolina Cavalry."[34]

This position was held until 11 o'clock that night, when Kilpatrick received orders to move to Two Taverns, on the Baltimore pike, about five miles southeast of Gettysburg, and some three miles due south from this place. It was 3 o'clock in the morning (Kilpatrick says daylight) when Custer's brigade went into bivouac at Two Taverns.[35]

One of the most singular, not to say amusing, things in Colonel Brooke-Rawle's oration, is the statement that Custer, "after his fight with the Confederate cavalry at Hunterstown, spent the night of July 2d in bivouac with the rest of the Third Division at Two Taverns."[36] Having had the honor to command the three companies of the Sixth Michigan Cavalry that were dismounted to the right of the road at Hunterstown, I remember distinctly that they were kept on that line until near midnight, when the division moved away; and I also remember well the weary night march, which lasted until the first streaks of dawn had begun to appear in the east. It was then, and not till then, that Custer's men were permitted to stretch their limbs upon the ground and snatch a brief rest, preparatory to the work of the coming day. The manner in which the Sixth Michigan Cavalry "spent the night" is pretty indelibly photographed upon the memory of every survivor who served with it in the Gettysburg campaign; and never

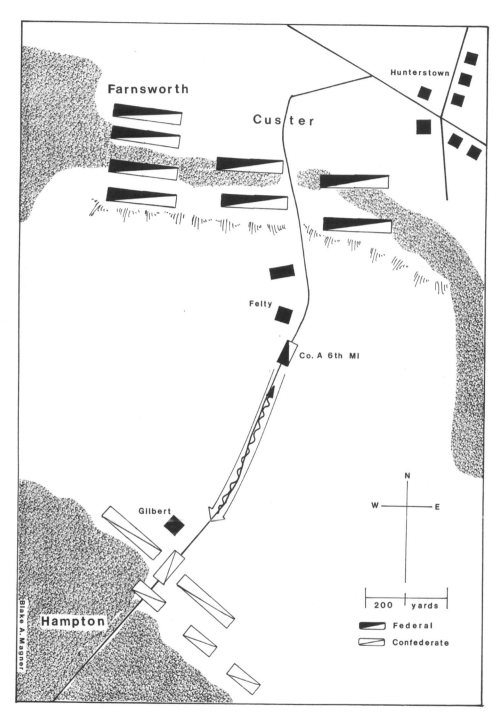

Farnsworth

Custer

Hunterstown

Felty

Co. A 6th MI

Gilbert

Hampton

Blake A. Magner

N
W — E
S

| 200 | yards |

Federal

Confederate

The Battle of Hunterstown, July 2, 1863

were the experiences of a single night less calculated to prepare soldiers
for the tremendous duties of the succeeding day, than were those which
the Michigan Brigade underwent on the night of July 2, 1863. From the
time when the Fifth and Sixth regiments left Emmittsburg on the afternoon of June 29th, they had hardly been given a moment for rest, and had
been in motion by night as well as by day. It may be surmised, therefore,
that Custer's men were not "fresh," if they were from "pastures green,"**
when, early on the morning of July 3d, they came upon this now historic
ground, ready and willing to do their part in the great conflict that was
impending.

The Second Division, which held this position on July 2d, as has been
seen, was withdrawn in the evening to the Baltimore pike, "to be available
for whatever duty they might be called upon to perform on the morrow."
On the morning of the 3d, Gregg was ordered to resume his position of
the day before, but states in his report that the First and Third brigades
(McIntosh[37] and Irvin Gregg[38]) were posted on the right of the infantry
about three-fourths of a mile nearer the Baltimore and Gettysburg pike,
because he learned that the Second Brigade (Custer's) of the Third Division was occupying his position of the day before. General Kilpatrick in his
report says: "At 11 P.M. (July 2d) received orders to move (from Hunterstown) to Two Taverns, which point we reached at daylight. At 8 A.M. (July
3d) received orders from headquarters Cavalry Corps to move to the left
of our line and attack the enemy's right and rear with my whole command,
and the reserve brigade. By some mistake General Custer's brigade was
ordered to report to General Gregg, and he (Custer) did not join me during the day."[39]

General Custer, in his report, gives the following, which is without
doubt the true explanation of the "mistake." He says:

> At an early hour on the morning of the 3d, I received an order through
> a staff officer of the brigadier general commanding the division (Kil-
> patrick) to move at once with my command and follow the First Bri-
> gade (Farnsworth) on the road leading from Two Taverns to Gettys-
> burg. Agreeably to the above instructions my column was formed and
> moved out on the road designated, when a staff officer of Brigadier
> General Gregg, commanding the Second Division, ordered me to take

**Colonel Brooke-Rawle, referring to Custer's brigade, employs this language.

my command and place it in position on the pike leading from York[††] (Hanover) to Gettysburg, which position formed the extreme right of our line of battle on that day.[40]

Thus it is made plain that there was no "mistake" about it. It was Gregg's prescience. He foresaw the risk of attempting to guard the right flank with only the two decimated brigades of his own division. With him, to see was to act. He took the responsibility of intercepting Kilpatrick's rear and largest brigade, turning it off the Baltimore pike to the right, instead of allowing it to go to the left as it had been ordered to do, and thus, doubtless, a serious disaster was averted. It makes us tremble to think of what might have been, of what inevitably must have happened had Gregg, with only the two little brigades of McIntosh and Irvin Gregg and Randol's battery, tried to cope single-handed with the four brigades and three batteries, comprising the very flower of the Confederate cavalry and artillery, which those brave knights—Stuart, Hampton and Fitzhugh Lee—were marshaling in person on Cress's ridge.[41] If Custer's presence on this field was opportune, and, as has often been said, providential, it is to General D. McM. Gregg to whom, under Providence, the credit for bringing him here is due. Gregg was a great and modest soldier; let us pause a moment before we enter upon a description of the coming battle, to pay to him the tribute of our admiration. In the light of all the official reports, put together link by link, so as to make one connected chain of evidence, we can see that the engagement which took place here almost twenty-six years ago, was, from first to last, a well planned battle, in which the different commands were maneuvered and placed with the same sagacity displayed by a skillful chess player in moving the pieces upon a chess board; in which every detail was the fruit of the brain of one man, who, from the time when he turned Custer to the northward until he set the First Michigan thundering against the brigades of Hampton and Fitzhugh Lee made not a single false move; who was distinguished not less for his intuitive foresight than for his quick perceptions at critical moments.

That man was General David McM. Gregg.

This conclusion has been reached by a mind not—certainly not—predisposed in that direction, after a careful recent study, and review of all the information within reach bearing upon that eventful day. If the Michigan

---

[††]Custer in his report reports the York for the Hanover Road.

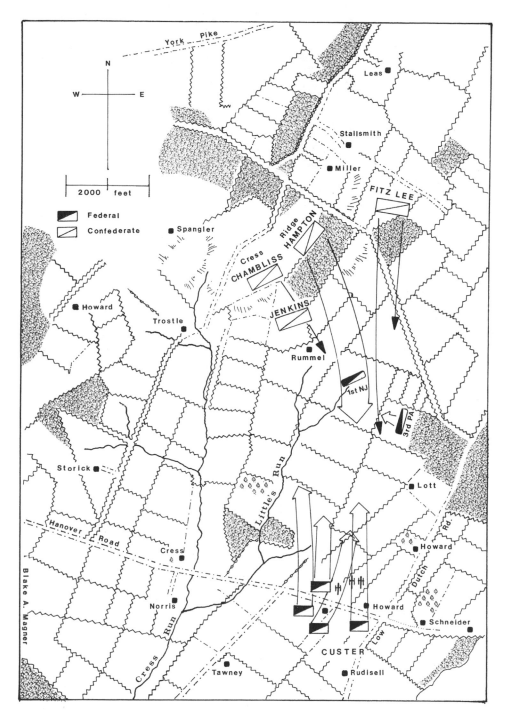

East Cavalry Field, Gettysburg, July 3, 1863

Brigade won honors here that will not perish, it was to Gregg that it owed the opportunity, and his guiding hand it was that made its blows effective. We shall see how, later in the day, he again boldly took responsibility at a critical moment and held Custer to his work on the right, even after the latter had been ordered by higher authority that he (Gregg), to rejoin Kilpatrick, and after Custer had begun the movement.

Now, having admitted, and, I think, demonstrated, how Gregg did the planning, let us briefly show how Custer and his brigade, for the greater part, at least, did the fighting.

Following the example of my predecessor in this field, I propose to halt and let Custer tell his own story up to a certain point, when the narrative will be resumed:

> Upon arriving at the point designated, I immediately placed my command in position, facing towards Gettysburg. At the same time I caused reconnaissances to be made on my front, right and rear, but failed to discover any considerable force of the enemy. Everything remained quiet until 10 A.M., when the enemy appeared on my right flank and opened upon me with a battery of six guns. Leaving two guns and a regiment to hold my first position and cover the road leading to Gettysburg, I shifted the remaining portion of my command, forming a new line of battle, at right angles to my former position. The enemy had obtained correct range of my new position, and was pouring solid shot and shell into my command with great accuracy. Placing two sections of Battery "M," Second Regular Artillery, in position, I ordered them to silence the enemy's battery, which order, notwithstanding the superiority of the enemy's position, was done in a very short space of time. My line, as it then existed, was shaped like the letter L. The shorter branch, formed of one section of Battery "M" (Clark's), supported by four squadrons of the Sixth Michigan Cavalry, faced towards Gettysburg, covering the pike; the long branch, compose of the two remaining sections of Battery "M," supported by a portion of the Sixth Michigan Cavalry on the left, and the First Michigan cavalry on the right—with the Seventh Michigan Cavalry still further to the right and in advance—was held in readiness to repel any attack on the Oxford (Low Dutch) road. The Fifth Michigan was dismounted and ordered to take position in front of center and left. The First Michigan was held in column of squadrons to observe the movements of the enemy, I ordered fifty men to be sent

one mile and a half on the Oxford[‡‡] (Low Dutch) road, and a detachment of equal size on the York (Hanover) road, both detachments being under command of the gallant Major Weber, who, from time to time, kept me so well informed of the movements of the enemy, that I was enabled to make my dispositions with complete success.[42]

General Custer says further, that, at twelve o'clock, he received an order directing him, on being relieved by a brigade of the Second Division, to move to the left and form a junction with Kilpatrick; that on the arrival of colonel McIntosh's brigade he prepared to execute the order; but, to quote his own language: "Before I had left my position, Brigadier General Gregg, commanding the Second Division, arrived with his entire command. Learning the true condition of affairs and rightly conjecturing that the enemy was making his dispositions for vigorously attacking our position, Brigadier General Gregg ordered me to remain in the position I then occupied."[43]

I have given so much space to these quotations because they cover a controverted point. It has been claimed, and General Gregg seems to countenance that view, that Custer was withdrawn, and that McIntosh, who was put in his place, opened the fight, after which Gregg brought Custer back to reinforce McIntosh. So far from this being true, it is just the reverse of the truth. Custer did not leave his position. The battle opened before the proposed change had taken place, and McIntosh was hurried in on the right of Custer. The fact is, the latter was reluctant to leave his post—knew he ought not to leave it. He had already been attacked by a fire from the artillery in position beyond the Rummel buildings. Major Weber, who was out on the cross road leading northwest from the Low Dutch road, had observed the movement of Stuart's column, headed by Chambliss and Jenkins,[44] past the Stallsmith farm to the wooded crest behind Rummel's and had reported it to Custer. Custer did indeed begin the movement. A portion of the Sixth Michigan and possibly of the Seventh, had been withdrawn, when he met Gregg coming on the field and explained to him the situation—that the enemy was "all around," and preparing to "push things." Gregg told him to remain where he was, and that portion of the brigade which was moving away halted, countermarched, and reoccupied its former position. The Fifth Michigan had not been withdrawn from the skirmish line, and

[‡‡]General Custer in his report erroneously speaks of the Hanover as the "York" Road, and the Low Dutch as the "Oxford."

Pennington's guns had never ceased to thunder their responses to the Confederate challenge.

Colonel Brooke-Rawle unwittingly endorses this view of the case; for, after having said in one part of his oration that "as soon as Custer, with his brigade, had moved off for the purpose of joining Kilpatrick near Round Top,"[45] he, later, goes on to say that "the Confederate battery now opened fire," and Pennington, who was still in position near the Spangler house, replied with promptness: It is absurd to suppose that Custer, "with his brigade," could be on the way to join Kilpatrick, while Pennington was "still in position," replying to the Confederate artillery. Battery "M" was as much a part of the Second Brigade, Third Division, as the Sixth Michigan cavalry, and Custer could not have been marching away, leaving Pennington "still in position."[46] No one claims that he was ordered to go with his cavalry only. General Gregg does not so state. There is then no room for any other conclusion than that Custer was to go, with his entire command, including the artillery. Pennington did not go—Colonel Rawle says he did not. No more did Colonel Alger or Colonel Town. The Sixth and Seventh moved a few rods away, but immediately returned before their position had been occupied by other troops. McIntosh was not in position on the right when the battle opened; for, according to the same authority still, after Pennington's reply to the Confederate battery, McIntosh had to send back for Randol's guns, which were not yet up. By Colonel Rawle's account, Pennington was playing a queer part—holding his position at the Spangler house without orders and without support, while his own brigade was marching away to Round Top. Custer, too, must be assumed to have overlooked the fact that he had a battery in his command, and to have gone off, leaving Pennington to decide for himself whether to remain and fight it out, or to limber to the rear in his own good time, and catch up with the cavalry by galloping across country, when the necessity for so doing should have been determined by his own sweet will.[§§]

Custer says, that the enemy opened upon him with a battery of six guns at 10 A.M. Stuart, on the contrary, claims to have left Gettysburg about noon. It is difficult to reconcile these two statements. A good deal of

---

[§§]Since the delivery of this address, I have received a letter from General D. McM. Gregg in which, after mentioning that he has read it, he says, "There is no conflict between your recollection and mine as to the events of that day."—J.H.K.

latitude may be given to the word "about," but it is probable that the one puts the hour too early, while the other does not give it early enough; for it is impossible that Custer could have been attacked until after the arrival of some portion of Stuart's command in the neighborhood of the battle-field.

As stated before, the official reports are often meagre [*sic*], if not misleading, and must be reinforced by the memoranda and recollections of participants before the exact truth will be known.

Major Charles E. Storrs,[47] who commanded a squadron of the Sixth Michigan, was sent out to the left and front of Custer's position soon after the brigade arrived upon the ground. He remained there several hours and was recalled about noon—he is positive it was later than 12 m.—to take position with the companies on the left of the battery. He states that the first shot was not fired till sometime after his recall, and he is sure it was not earlier than 2 o'clock.***

When Stuart left Gettysburg, as he says, about noon, he took with him Chambliss, and Jenkins' brigades of cavalry and Griffin's[48] battery. Hampton and Fitzhugh Lee were to follow; also, Breathed's[49] and McGregor's[50] batteries, as soon as the latter had replenished their ammunition chests. Stuart moved two and a half miles out on the York turnpike, when he turned to the right by a country road that runs southeasterly past the Stallsmith farm. (This road intersects the Low Dutch road, about three-fourths of a mile from where the latter crosses the Hanover pike.) Turning off from this road to the right, Stuart posted the brigades of Jenkins and Chambliss, and Griffin's battery, on the commanding Cress' ridge, beyond Rummel's and more than a mile from the position occupied by Custer. This movement was noticed by Major Weber, who, with his detachment of the Sixth Michigan Cavalry, was stationed in the woods northeast of Rummel's, where he could look out upon the open country beyond, and he promptly reported the fact to Custer.

The first shot that was fired came from near the edge of the woods beyond Rummel's. According to Major McClellan, who was Assistant Adjutant General on Stuart's staff,[51] this was from a section of Griffin's battery, and was aimed at random by Stuart himself, he not knowing whether there was anything in his front or not. Several shots were fired in this way.

***Since writing the above a possible solution of this difficulty has come to my mind. It is this: That General Custer originally wrote "1 o'clock" and that in copying his report the "1" and the "o" were mistaken for "10" and the "o'clock" added.

Major McClellan is doubtless right in this, that these shots were fired as feelers; but it is to me inconceivable that Stuart should have been totally unaware of the presence of any Federal force in his immediate front; that he should not have known that there was stationed on the opposite ridge a brigade of cavalry and a battery. Gregg had been there the day before, and Stuart must at least have suspected, if he did not know, that he would find him there again. It is probable that he fired the shots in the hope of drawing out and developing the force that he knew was there, to ascertain how formidable it might be and how great the obstacle in the way of his further progress towards the rear of the union lines.

The information he sought was promptly furnished.

It was then that Custer put Pennington's battery in position; and the three sections of rifled cannon opened with a fire so rapid and accurate that Griffin was speedily silenced and compelled to leave the field.

Then there was a lull. I cannot say how long it lasted, but during its continuance General Gregg arrived and took command in person. About this time, also, it was safe to say, that Hampton and Fitzhugh Lee came up and took position on the left of Chambliss and Jenkins. The Confederate line then extended clear across the Federal front, and was screened by the two patches of woods between Rummel's and the Stallsmith farm.

A battalion of the Sixth Michigan Cavalry, of which mine was the leading squadron, was placed in support and on the left of Pennington's battery. This formed, at first, the short line of the L referred to in Custer's report; but it was subsequently moved farther to the right and faced in the same general direction as the rest of the line, where it remained until the battle ended. Its duty there was to repel any attempt that might be made to capture the battery.

The ground upon which these squadrons were stationed overlooked the plain, and the slightest demonstration in open ground from either side was immediately discernible. From this vantage ground it was possible to see every phase of the magnificent contest that followed. It was like a spectacle, arranged for us to see. We were in the position of spectators at joust or tournament, where the knights, advancing from their respective sides, charge full tilt upon each other in the middle of the field.

The lull of which I have spoken was like the calm that precedes the storm. The troopers were dismounted, standing "in place rest" in front of their horses, when suddenly there burst upon the air the sound of that terrific cannonading that preceded Pickett's charge. The earth quaked. The tremendous volume of sound volleyed and rolled across the intervening hills like reverberating thunder in a storm.

It was then between 1 and 2 P.M. (Major Storrs says after 2). It was not long thereafter when General Custer directed Colonel Alger to advance and engage the enemy. The Fifth Michigan, its flanks protected by a portion of the Sixth Michigan on the left, by Macintosh's brigade on the right, moved briskly forward under its gallant and zealous commander towards the wooded screen, behind which the enemy was known to be concealed. In this movement the right of regiment was swung well forward, the left somewhat "refused," so that Colonel Alger's line was very nearly at right angles with the left of Stuart's position. As the Fifth Michigan advanced from field to field and fence to fence, a line of gray came out from behind the Rummel buildings and the woods beyond.

A stubborn and spirited contest ensued. The opposing batteries filled the air with shot and shrieking shell. Amazing marksmanship was shown by Pennington's battery, and such accurate artillery firing was never seen on any other field. Alger's men, with their eight-shotted carbines, forced their adversaries slowly but surely back, the gray line fighting well, and superior in numbers, but unable to withstand the storm of bullets. It made a final stand behind the strong line of fences in front of Rummel's and a few hundred yards out from the foot of the slope whereon Stuart's reserves were posted. While the fight was raging on the plain, Weber, with his outpost, was driven in. His two companies were added to the four already stationed on the left of Pennington's battery. Weber, who had been promoted to Major but a few days before, was ordered by Colonel Gray to assume command of the battalion. As he took his place in front of the leading squadron he said: "I have seen thousands of rebels over yonder," pointing to the front; "The country over there is full of them." He had observed all of Stuart's movements, and it was he who gave Custer the first important information as to what the enemy was doing; which information was transmitted to Gregg, and possibly had a determining influence in keeping Custer on the field.

Weber was a born soldier. Although but twenty-two years of age, he had seen much service. A private in the Third Michigan infantry in 1861, he was next battalion adjutant of the Second Michigan Cavalry, served on the staff of General Elliott in the southwest, and came home with Alger to take a troop in the Sixth Cavalry in 1862. The valuable service performed by him at Gettysburg was fitly recognized by Custer in official report. He was killed ten days later at Falling Waters, while leading his squadron of the Sixth Michigan in a charge which was described by Kilpatrick as the "most gallant ever made." Anticipating a spirited fight, he was eager to have a part in it. "Bob," he said to me a few days before, while marching through Maryland, "I want a chance to make one saber charge." He thought the time had come. His eye flashed and his face flushed as he watched the progress of the fight, fretting and chafing to be held in reserve while the bugle was summoning others to the charge.

But the Fifth Michigan, holding the most advanced position, suffered greatly, Hampton having reinforced the Confederate line, Major N. H. Ferry[53] being among the killed. Repeating rifles are not only effective but wasteful weapons as well, and, at last, Colonel Alger, finding that his ammunition had given out, felt compelled to retire his regiment and seek his horses. Seeing this, the enemy's line sprang forward with a yell. The union line was seen to yield. The puffs of smoke from the muzzles of their guns had almost ceased. It was plain that they were out of ammunition and, for that reason, unable to maintain the contest longer. On from field to field, the line of gray followed in exultant pursuit. Breathed and McGregor opened with redoubled violence. Shells dropped and exploded among the skirmishers, while thicker and faster they fell around the position of the reserves on the ridge. Pennington replied with astonishing effect, for every shot hit the mark, and the opposing artillerists were unable to silence a single Union gun. But still they came, until it seemed that nothing could stop their victorious career. "Men, be ready," said Weber; "we will have to charge that line." But the course of the pursuit took it towards the right, in the direction of Randol's battery, where Chester[54] was serving out canister with the same liberal hand displayed by Pennington's Lieutenants, Clark,[55] Woodruff,[56] and Hamilton.[57]

Just then a column of mounted men was seen advancing from our right and rear, squadron succeeding squadron, until an entire regiment came into view, with sabers gleaming and colors gaily fluttering in the breeze. It was the Seventh Michigan, commanded by Colonel Mann. Gregg, seeing the necessity for prompt action, had ordered it to charge. As it moved forward and cleared the battery. Custer drew his saber, placing himself in front, and shouted, "Come on, you Wolverines!" The Seventh dashed into an open field and rode straight at the dismounted line, which, staggered by the appearance of this new foe, broke to the rear and ran for its reserves. Custer led the charge half way across the plain, then turned to the left; but the gallant regiment swept on under its own leaders, riding down and capturing many prisoners.

There was no check to the charge. The squadrons kept on in good form. Every man yelled at the top of his voice until the regiment had gone, probably, 1,000 yard straight toward the Confederate batteries, when, by some error of the guide of the leading squadron, the head of column was deflected to the left, making a quarter turn, and the regiment was hurled headlong against a post and rail fence that ran obliquely in front of the Rummel barn. This proved for the moment an impassable barrier. The squadrons coming up successively at a charge, rushed pell mell upon each other and were thrown into a state of indescribable confusion; though the rear companies, without order or orders, formed left and right front into line along the fence and pluckily began firing across it into the faces of the Confederates, who, when they saw the impetuous onset of the Seventh thus abruptly checked, rallied and began to collect in swarms upon the opposite side. Some of the officers leaped from their saddles and called upon the men to assist in making an opening. Among these were Colonel George G. Briggs,[58] then adjutant, and Captain H. N. Moore.[59] The task was a difficult and hazardous one, the posts and rails being so firmly united that it could be accomplished only by lifting the posts, which were deeply set, and removing several lengths at once. This was finally done, however, though the regiment was exposed, not only to a fire from the force in front, but to a flanking fire from a strong skirmish line along a fence to the right and running nearly at right-angles with one through which it was trying to pass.

While this was going on, Brigg's horse was shot and he found himself on foot, with three Confederate prisoners on his hands. With these he started to the rear, having no remount. Before he could reach a place of safety the rush of charging squadrons from either side had intercepted his retreat. In the melee that followed, two of his men ran away; the other undertook the duty of escorting his captor back to the Confederate lines. The experiment cost him his life, but the plucky adjutant, although he did not run away, lived to fight again on many another day.

In the meantime, through the passageway thus effected, the regiment moved forward, the center squadron leading, and resumed the charge. The Confederates once more fell back before it. The charge was continued across a plowed field to the front and right, up to and past Rummel's to a point within 200 or 300 yards of the Confederate battery. There another fence was encountered, the last one in the way of reaching the battery, the guns of which were pouring canister into the charging column as fast as they could fire. Two men, Privates Powers[60] and Ingelede,[61] of Captain Moore's company, leaped this fence and passed several rods beyond. Powers came back without a scratch, but Ingelede was severely wounded. These two men were certainly within 200 yards of the enemy's cannon.

But seeing that the enemy to the right had thrown down the fences, and were forming a column for a charge, the companies of the Seventh fell back through the opening in the fence. Captain Moore, in whose company sixteen horses had been killed, retired slowly, endeavoring to cover the retreat of his dismounted men, but, taking the wrong direction, came to the fence one hundred yards above the opening, just as the enemy's charging column struck him. Glancing over his shoulder, he caught the gleam of a saber thrust from the arm of a sturdy Confederate. He ducked to avoid the blow, but received the point on the back of his head. At the same time a pistol ball crashed through his charger's brain and the horse went down, Moore's leg under him. An instant later Moore avenged his steed with the last shot in his revolver, and the Confederate fell dead at his side. Some dismounted men of the Thirteenth Virginia Cavalry[62] took Moore prisoner and escorted him back to the rear of their battery, from which position, during the excitement that followed, he made his escape.

But now Alger, who, when his ammunition gave out, hastened to his horses, had succeeded in mounting one battalion, commanded by Major L. S. Trowbridge;[63] and when the Ninth and Thirteenth Virginia struck the flank of the Seventh Michigan, he ordered that officer to charge and meet this new danger. Trowbridge and his men dashed forward with a cheer, and the enemy in their turn were put to flight. Past the Rummel building, through the fields, almost to the fence where Moore had halted, Trowbridge kept on; but he too, was obliged to retire before the destructive fire of the Confederate cannon, which did not cease to belch forth destruction upon every detachment of the Union cavalry that approached near enough to threaten them. The Major's horse was killed, but his orderly was close at hand with another and he escaped. When his battalion was retiring, it also was assailed in flank by a mounted charge of the First Virginia Cavalry,[64] which was met and driven back by the other battalion of the Fifth Michigan, led by Colonel Alger.

Then, as it seemed, the two belligerent forces paused to get their second breath. Up to the time the battle had raged with varying fortune.

Victory, that appeared about to perch first on one banner than on the other, held aloof, as if disdaining to favor either. The odds, indeed, had been rather with the Confederates than against them, for Stuart managed to outnumber his adversary at every critical point, though Gregg forced the fighting, putting Stuart on his defense and checkmating his plan to fight an offensive battle. But the wily Confederate had kept his two choicest brigades in reserve for the supreme moment, intending then to throw them into the contest and sweep the field with one grand, resistless charge.

All felt that the time for this effort had come, when a body of mounted men began to emerge from the woods and form column to the left as they debouched in the open field. Squadron after squadron, regiment after regiment, orderly as if on parade, came into view, and successively took their places.

Then Pennington opened with all his guns. Six rifled pieces, as fast as they could fire, rained shot and shell into that fated column. The effect was deadly. Great gaps were torn in that mass of mounted men, but the rents were quickly closed. Men and horses were shot away, but others took their places. Then they were ready. Confederate chroniclers tell us there were two brigades—eight regiments, under their own favorite leaders. In the van floated a stand of colors. It was the battle-flag of Wade Hampton, who, with Fitzhugh Lee, was leading the assaulting column. In superb form, with sabers glistening, they advanced. The men on foot gave way to let them pass. It was an inspiring and imposing spectacle, that brought a murmur of admiration from the spectators on the opposite ridge. Pennington double-shotted his guns with canister, and the head of the column staggered under each murderous discharge. But still it advanced, led on by an imperturable spirit that no storm of war could cow.

Meantime Alger, with his Fifth, had drawn aside a little to the left, making ready to spring. McIntosh's squadrons were in the edge of the opposite woods. The Seventh was sullenly retiring, with faces to the foe. On and on, nearer and nearer, came the assaulting column, charging straight for Randol's battery. The storm of canister caused them to waver a little, but that was all. A few moments would bring them among the guns of Chester, who, like Pennington's lieutenants, was still firing with frightful regularity as fast as he could load. Then Gregg rode over to the First Michigan and directed Town to charge. Custer dashed up with similar instructions, and as Town ordered sabers to be drawn, placed himself by his side, in front of the leading squadron.

With ranks well closed, with guidons flying and bugles sounding, the grand old regiment of veterans, led by Town and Custer, moved forward to meet that host, outnumbering it three to one; first at a trot, then the command to charge rang out, and, with gleaming saber and flashing pistol, Town and his heroes were hurled right into the teeth of Hampton and Fitzhugh Lee. Alger, who with the Fifth had been waiting for the right moment, charged in on the right flank of the column as it passed, as some of McIntosh's squadrons did on its left. One company of the Seventh, under Lieutenant Dan Littlefield,[65] also joined in the charge.

Then it was steel to steel and Greek met Greek. For minutes—and for minutes that seemed like years—the gray column stood and staggered before the blow; then yielded and fled. Alger and McIntosh had pierced its flanks, but Town's impetuous charge in front went through it like a wedge, splitting it in twain and scattering the Confederate horsemen in disorderly rout back to the woods whence they came.

During this last melee the brazen lips of the cannon were dumb. It was a fierce hand to hand encounter between the Michigan men and the flower of the Southern cavaliers, led by their favorite commanders, in which the latter were worsted.

Stuart retreated to his stronghold, leaving the Union forces in possession of the field.

The rally sounded, the lines were reformed, the wounded cared for, and everything made ready for a renewal of the conflict. But the charge of the First Michigan ended the cavalry fighting on the right at Gettysburg. Military critics have pronounced it the finest charges made during the war.

It was a famous fight and a bloody one. Custer's brigade lost one officer and twenty-eight men killed, eleven officers and 112 men wounded, sixty-seven men missing; total loss, 219. Gregg's division lost one man killed, seven officers and nineteen men wounded, eight men missing; total, thirty-five. In other words, while Gregg's division, two brigades, lost thirty-five, Custer's single brigade suffered a loss of 219. These figures apply only to the fight on July 3d.[†††]

[†††]Colonel Brooke-Rawle gives an exaggerated estimate of the losses for which there is no verification in the official records. The above figures are taken from the volume of the Rebellion record, published since this paper was written, an advanced copy of which was kindly furnished to my by Colonel H. M. Lazelle and Major Geo. B. Davis, of the War Records Office.—J.H.K.

I find from the official records that the brigade during the three days, July 1st, 2d and 3d, lost one officer and thirteen men killed, thirteen officers and 134 men wounded, seventy-eight men missing; total, 257. It is difficult, however, to get the full figures, for regimental commanders did not make their reports on the same basis. The above compilation gives the Sixth Michigan only one man missing—a manifest absurdity, unless "missing" is construed to mean those, only, who could be accounted for in no other way. This rule, evidently, all did not follow. Had the Sixth Michigan been given its proper credit for "missing in action," the total loss would be still greater than it appears from the figures given.

The operations of the Michigan Cavalry Brigade in the Gettysburg campaign, properly began at Gettysburg June 28th, and ended at Falling Waters July 14th, or perhaps a little later, when the pursuit of Lee beyond the river ceased. Any sketch that does not cover the entire period, will fall short of doing justice to Custer and his command. But, to pursue the subject further at this time, would be to violate the proprieties and abuse the patience of my hearers, if, indeed I have not done so already. I would like to go on and speak of the pursuit on July 4th; of the midnight battle in the mountains at Monterey;[66] of the fight at Boonesborough,[67] and the bloody affairs at Hagerstown,[68] Williamsport[69] and Falling Waters;[70] to tell the story of the death of Weber and Jewett,[71] of Royce,[72] Bolza,[73] Elliott,[74] McElhenny,[75] and Snyder,[76] and all the noble men who fell with them during those last few eventful days. But this must be done, if at all, on some future occasion. Suffice it to say that during the period named the brigade lost thirty officers killed and wounded, whose names are here given.

Killed.
First Michigan—Captain W. R. Elliott, Captain C. J. Snyder,
    Lieutenant J. S. McElhenny—3.
Fifth Michigan—Major N. H. Ferry—1.
Sixth Michigan—Major P. A. Weber, Captain, D. G. Royce,
    Lieutenant C. E. Bolza, Adjutant A. C. Jewett—4.

Wounded.
First Michigan—Captain D. W. Clemmer,[77] Lieutenant E. F.
    Bicker,[78] Captain A. W. Duggan,[79] Captain H. E Hascall,[80]
    Captain W. M. Heazlett,[81] Captain G. R. Maxwell,[82] Lieutenant
    R. N. Van Atter[83]—7.

Fifth Michigan—Colonel R. A. Alger, Lieutenant Colonel E.
 Gould,[84] Lieutenant T. J. Dean,[85] Lieutenant G. N Dutcher[86]—4.
Sixth Michigan—Lieutenant G. W. Crawford,[87] Captain H. E.
 Thompson, Captain J. H. Kidd, Lieutenant E. Potter,[88] Lieutenant
 S. Shipman[89]—5.
Seventh Michigan—Lieutenant J. G. Birney,[90] Lieutenant J. L.
 Carpenter,[91] Lieutenant E. Gray,[92] Lieutenant C. Griffith,[93]
 Captain Alex. Walker[94]—5.

It has not been possible for me to obtain a list of the men killed and
wounded for that particular period. The record, however, shows that the
four regiments during their entire time of service, lost twenty-three officers and 328 men killed; eight officers and 111 men died of wounds; nine
officers and 991 men died of disease; a grand total of 1,470 men, who gave
up their lives during those four awful years. This does not include those
who have died since the war from the effects of wounds and sickness, im-
prisonment and privations incurred while in the line of duty.

Colonel Fox's history of the casualties in the war shows that there were
260 cavalry regiments in the Union service during the War of the Rebellion. Of all these, the First Michigan lost the largest number of men killed
in action, with one exception—the First Maine. In percentage of killed, in
proportion to the number of men engaged, the Fifth and Sixth Michigan
rank all the rest, not excepting the two first named; and it must be remembered that the Fifth and Sixth went out in 1862, and did their first fighting
in the campaign which we have now been considering. They also stood
third and fourth respectively, in the number of killed, being ranked in that
respect by the First Maine and First Michigan alone.

Comrades: This is a record to be proud of. No man will ever blush to
own that he was one of Custer's Michigan troopers. Their record is written
in history, where it will have a permanent as well as an honorable place. As
we stand here to-day, within the shadow of a beautiful monument erected
to commemorate the courage and patriotism of the men whose fortitude
helped to save the Union right, let us renew our fealty to the cause for
which they fought, and resolve that in the years that are left to us we will be
loyal to ourselves, true to the manhood that was here put to the proof—
true as were those noble dead who gave their lives for the Union.

NOTES

1. Kidd refers to the command of Brig. Gen. David McMurtrie Gregg, which was the Second Division, Cavalry Corps, Army of the Potomac.

2. The speech commemorating the dedication of the monument to the 3d Pennsylvania Cavalry of Gregg's division was given by Lt. Col. William Brooke-Rawle, who fought on the East Cavalry Field as a lieutenant. An abridged version of that speech was later published in the *Philadelphia Weekly Times* and reprinted in a collection of articles from the *Times*. To find the text of this speech, see William Brooke-Rawle, "The Cavalry Fight on the Right Flank at Gettysburg," *Annals of the War* (reprint, Secaucus, N.J.: Blue and Grey Press, 1996), 467–84. The full text of Brooke-Rawle's speech appears in the regimental history of the 3d Pennsylvania Cavalry; see William Brooke-Rawle, ed., *History of the Third Pennsylvania Cavalry, Sixtieth Regiment Pennsylvania Volunteers, in the American Civil War, 1861–1865* (Philadelphia: Franklin Printing Co., 1905), 261–91.

3. Maj. Gen. James Ewell Brown "Jeb" Stuart, commander of the Confederate cavalry forces attached to the Army of Northern Virginia from 1862 to 1864.

4. Brig. Gen. Wade Hampton, commander of a brigade under Stuart. Hampton succeeded Stuart in command of the Army of Northern Virginia's cavalry after Stuart's death in May 1864. Hampton was promoted to major general in early 1864 and to lieutenant general later that year.

5. Brig. Gen. Fitzhugh Lee, nephew of Robert E. Lee and commander of a brigade of cavalry under Stuart. He eventually was promoted to major general and assumed command of a division.

6. The horse artillery battery of Lt. Alexander C. M. Pennington, Battery M. 2d U.S. Artillery.

7. Kidd refers to the great cannonade prior to the stepping off of the Pickett-Pettigrew-Trimble infantry attack on the afternoon of July 3.

8. Col. Russell A. Alger, commanding officer of the 5th Michigan Cavalry.

9. A brutal and bloody cavalry engagement took place at Hawe's Shop, Virginia on May 28, 1864. As Kidd points out, a mounted charge by the Michigan Cavalry Brigade rescued Gregg's Second Division from sure destruction.

10. Brig. Gen. Hugh Judson Kilpatrick, commander of the 3d Cavalry Division, Cavalry Corps, Army of the Potomac. This is the division that the Michigan Cavalry Brigade was assigned to serve in.

11. The portion of Kilpatrick's report referred to by Kidd appears in *War of the Rebellion: A Compilation of the Official Records of the Union and Confederate Armies*, 128 volumes (Washington, D.C.: GPO, 1880–1901), series 1, vol. 27, 1:992–93 (hereafter, unless otherwise noted, all future *OR* references will be to series 1).

12. Brig. Gen. Joseph Tarr Copeland was a prominent lawyer and judge in Michigan. At the outbreak of the Civil War, he was commissioned lieutenant colonel in the 1st Michigan Cavalry. In 1862 he was given authority to raise a regiment of mounted infantry that became known as Copeland's Mounted Rifles, which eventually became the 5th Michigan Cavalry,

and was armed with Spencer seven-shot repeating rifles. Copeland, commissioned colonel in August 1861, was promoted to brigadier general of volunteers on November 29, 1862. When the Michigan Cavalry Brigade was formed in the spring of 1863, he was given command of the brigade, serving until his relief from command on June 28, 1863. Copeland was probably treated unjustly in being relieved of his command. For more information, see Ezra J. Warner, *Generals in Blue* (Baton Rouge: Louisiana State University Press, 1964), 92–93.

13. Granger went on to become a brevet major general of volunteers and accomplished corps commander with the Army of the Cumberland, serving in the Western Theater. Warner, *Generals in Blue*, 181.

14. Philip H. Sheridan would eventually become general in chief of the armies of the United States. A protégé of Ulysses S. Grant, the aggressive Irish cavalryman would lead the Army of the Potomac's Cavalry Corps to glory in 1864–65.

15. Col. Thornton F. Brodhead, a prominent attorney and Mexican war hero.

16. Col. Charles H. Town, who succeeded Brodhead in command of the 1st Michigan Cavalry.

17. Maj. Gen. Julius Stahel, a Hungarian-born cavalry officer who commanded the independent division of cavalry assigned to the defenses of Washington, D.C., of which the Michigan Cavalry Brigade was originally assigned. Kidd described Stahel, who was an officer of marginal talent, as a "dapper little Dutchman."

18. A prominent spot for crossing the Potomac River, Edwards Ferry is near Leesburg, Virginia, where Goose Creek empties into the Potomac. Much of the Army of the Potomac crossed the river here on its way north into Pennsylvania.

19. Maj. Gen. John Fulton Reynolds, of Pennsylvania, was generally considered the finest subordinate commander in the Army of the Potomac, and he had turned down army command early in June. On July 1, 1863, while commanding the left wing of the Army of the Potomac, Reynolds was killed in action.

20. At the time of the Gettysburg campaign, Alger was a colonel. He received a brevet promotion to brigadier general effective March 13, 1865.

21. The Army of the Potomac's First Cavalry Division consisted of three brigades and was the largest of the three divisions assigned to the Cavalry Corps. Two of its brigades performed admirably at Gettysburg on July 1, holding off an entire division of Confederate infantry for several hours that morning. For additional information, see Eric J. Wittenberg, "John Buford in the Gettysburg Campaign," *Gettysburg: Articles of Lasting Historical Interest* 11 (July 1994): 1–36.

22. Kentucky-born Brig. Gen. John Buford commanded the 1st Cavalry Division. A member of West Point's class of 1848, Buford was a hard-bitten Regular who had spent his entire career in the mounted service. Considered by many of his peers to be the finest cavalry officer in Federal service, Buford died of typhoid fever on December 16, 1863. He was promoted to major general on his deathbed to honor his outstanding performance at Gettysburg on the first day of the battle.

23. Maj. Gen. John Pope commanded the Army of Virginia, which suffered a terrible defeat at Second Bull Run, August 28–30, 1862.

24. Brodhead received a mortal wound while leading a mounted charge of the 1st Michigan Cavalry at the Lewis Ford, the closing engagement of the Second Battle of Bull Run. Brodhead received a posthumous brevet to brigadier general for his gallantry at the Lewis Ford.

25. Col. John Chambliss of the 13th Virginia Cavalry was the senior colonel in the cavalry division of Brig. Gen. William H. F. "Rooney" Lee, son of Gen. Robert E. Lee. When Rooney Lee was badly wounded at the Battle of Brandy Station on June 9, 1863, Chambliss, as senior regimental colonel, assumed command of Lee's brigade. He commanded it throughout the Gettysburg campaign.

26. Brig. Gen. Elon J. Farnsworth of Illinois was promoted from captain to brigadier general of volunteers on June 28, 1863. Assigned to command of the 1st Brigade of the Third Division, Farnsworth performed admirably at the Battle of Hanover on June 30, 1863, and at the Battle of Hunterstown on July 2. Ordered by Kilpatrick to lead a hopeless and futile mounted charge against infantry in position after the repulse of Pickett's Charge on the afternoon of July 3, Farnsworth was killed while leading his troopers. An officer of great promise, his career was snuffed out too early. For a detailed analysis of Farnsworth's charge and death, see, Eric J. Wittenberg, *Gettysburg's Forgotten Cavalry Actions* (Gettysburg: Thomas Publications, 1998).

27. Capt. Henry E. Thompson of Grand Rapids, Michigan, and commander of Co. A of the 6th Michigan Cavalry. A fine officer in his own right, Thompson, a close friend of Kidd's, received a brevet to brigadier general of volunteers on March 13, 1865.

28. Lt. Edward Potter, Co. C, of Burtchville.

29. Maj. Peter A. Weber, of Grand Rapids, was considered by many to be the finest officer in the regiment. Weber was killed leading a mounted charge against Confederate infantry at Falling Waters, Maryland, on July 14, 1863, during the retreat from Gettysburg.

30. Kidd was incorrect about the weapons carried by the 5th Michigan at this time. In fact, the 5th Michigan was armed with longer barreled Spencer repeating rifles. They would not receive Spencer carbines until the spring of 1864.

31. Maj. Gen. George B. McClellan, a member of the legendary West Point class of 1846, is generally considered the officer most responsible for forging the Army of the Potomac into a formidable fighting force. Beloved by the men who served under his command, he was commonly known as "Little Mac."

32. 1st Lt. Stephen H. Ballard of Grand Rapids. Captured at Hunterstown on July 2, he was held as a prisoner of war until released on March 1, 1865.

33. *OR*, vol. 27, 1:992.

34. Ibid., 2:724. Hampton's brigade consisted of the 1st North Carolina, 1st South Carolina, 2d South Carolina, Cobb's Legion, Phillips Legion, and Jeff Davis Legion.

35. Ibid., 1:992.

36. Brooke-Rawle, *History of the Third Pennsylvania Cavalry*, 269.

37. Col. John B. McIntosh, of the 3d Pennsylvania Cavalry, commander of the 1st Brigade, 2d Cavalry Division, Cavalry Corps, Army of the Potomac.

38. Col. John Irvin Gregg, first cousin of David M. Gregg, of the 16th Pennsylvania Cavalry, commander of the 3d Brigade, 2d Cavalry Division, Cavalry Corps, Army of the Potomac.

39. *OR*, vol. 27, 1:992–93.

40. For some reason, Custer's comprehensive report of the Gettysburg campaign did not make it into the *Official Records* as published by the War Department. A lengthy report by Custer was omitted for unknown reasons. However, it was included, largely verbatim, in an early biography of Custer by Frederick Whitaker, *A Complete Life of General Custer*, 2 vols. (New York: Sheldon and Co., 1876), 1:174–76. (Quote appears on page 174.)

41. This is the prominent ridge that is the high point of the East Cavalry Field battlefield. Some accounts spell it as "Kress's Ridge."

42. Whitaker, *Complete Life*, 175.

43. Ibid., 176.

44. Kidd refers here to the brigade of Brig. Gen. Albert Gallatin Jenkins. Jenkins had been badly wounded on July 2, and his troopers were under command of Lt. Col. Vincent Witcher of the 34th Battalion of Virginia Cavalry on July 3.

45. Brooke-Rawle, *Third Pennsylvania Cavalry*, 273.

46. Ibid., 273–74.

47. Maj. Charles E. Storrs of Blendon, Michigan.

48. Capt. William H. Griffin's Maryland Battery of Stuart's Horse Artillery Battalion.

49. Capt. James Breathed's Virginia Battery of Stuart's Horse Artillery Battalion.

50. Capt. William McGregor's Virginia Battery of Stuart's Horse Artillery Battalion.

51. Maj. Henry B. McClellan, of Philadelphia, a first cousin of Union major general George B. McClellan, served as Stuart's assistant adjutant general. McClellan wrote a fine memoir of his service with Stuart, and the account that Kidd references appears there. See Henry B. McClellan, *I Rode With Jeb Stuart: The Life and Campaigns of Major-General J.E.B. Stuart* (Bloomington: University of Indiana Press, 1958), 338.

52. Kidd is in error here. The Spencer rifle had a seven-shot magazine, not eight.

53. Maj. Noah H. Ferry of White River, Michigan, of the 5th Michigan Cavalry.

54. Lt. James Chester, a fine soldier breveted for gallantry twice in the Civil War, including once for the fight on the East Cavalry Field. Chester eventually achieved the rank of major in the Regular Army, a high rank for a nineteeth-century artillerist.

55. Lt. Robert Clarke, of Pennsylvania. For a fine capsule review of the history of Pennington's Battery, see James A. Morgan III, *Always Ready, Always Willing: Battery M, Second U.S. Artillery* (Gaithersburg, Md.: Olde Soldier Books, n.d.).

56. Lt. Carle A. Woodruff, another career artillerist who achieved the rank of brigadier general in the Regular Army after a forty-two-year career. Woodruff received a brevet to captain for his gallant service during the East Cavalry Field fight.

57. Lt. Frank B. Hamilton, a member of West Point's class of 1862, received a brevet to captain for his service in the East Cavalry Field fight.

58. A lieutenant at the time of the Battle of Gettysburg, Briggs, by then a lieutenant colonel, accepted the surrender flag at Appomattox on April 9, 1865.

59. Capt. Herman N. Moore of Grand Rapids, commanding Co. K, 7th Michigan Cavalry.

60. This could be either Pvt. Narvy Powers or Pvt. William C. Powers, both of whom served in Co. K and were apparently present at the Battle of Gettysburg.

61. Kidd apparently means Pvt. Eber E. Ingledue of Carmel, Michigan.

62. One of the units of Chambliss's Brigade, heavily engaged with the Michigan Cavalry Brigade.

63. Maj. Luther S. Trowbridge, a fine officer who received a brevet to brigadier general of volunteers on March 13, 1865.

64. One of the regiments of Fitz Lee's brigade.

65. Lt. Daniel W. Littlefield of Kent County, who served with Co. I of the 7th Michigan Cavalry.

66. At midnight on the night of July 4–5, 1863, a brutal midnight fight occurred in the Monterey Pass between a small contingent of Confederate cavalry and Kilpatrick's division. For more information on this fight, see Eric J. Wittenberg, "The Midnight Fight in the Monterey Pass, July 4–5, 1863," *North and South*, 2.6 (August 1999), 44–54.

67. The Federal cavalry corps had a severe engagement at Boonsboro, Maryland, on July 8.

68. Kilpatrick's division was defeated by Confederate cavalry at Hagerstown, Maryland, on July 6.

69. After withdrawing from Hagerstown on July 6, Kilpatrick's division joined Buford's First Division in fighting at Williamsport. The combined Federal force was defeated by a scratch force of Confederates under command of Brig. Gen. John D. Imboden.

70. At Falling Waters, Maryland, on July 14, Kilpatrick and Buford pitched into the Confederate rear as Lee's army crossed the Potomac River. The rash charge killed Confederate brigadier general James J. Pettigrew and led to the capture of nearly an entire infantry brigade. Had there been better coordination between Kilpatrick and Buford, the attack would have been even more successful. Kidd was badly wounded in the foot during this fight.

71. Lt. Aaron C. Jewett of Ann Arbor, killed in action at Williamsport, Maryland, on July 6.

72. Capt. David G. Royce of Burns, killed in action at Falling Waters.

73. Lt. Charles E. Bolza of Grand Rapids, killed in action at Falling Waters.

74. Capt. William R. Elliott of Co. C of the 1st Michigan Cavalry, killed in action at Monetery Pass.

75. Lt. James S. McElhenny of Co. G of the 1st Michigan Cavalry, killed in action at Monterey Pass.

76. Capt. Charles F. Snyder of Co. F of the 1st Michigan Cavalry, mortally wounded at the Battle of Hagerstown on July 6, died of his wounds on July 19.

77. Capt. David W. Clemmer of Co. K.

78. Unable to identify.

79. Capt. Andrew W. Duggan of Co. B, 1st Michigan Cavalry.

80. Capt. Herman E. Hascall of Co. E, 1st Michigan Cavalry, wounded in the fighting on the East Cavalry Field on July 3, 1863.

81. Capt. William M. Heazlit of Co. M, 1st Michigan Cavalry, also wounded on the East Cavalry Field.

82. Lt. George R. Maxwell of Co. E , 1st Michigan Cavalry, wounded in the fighting at the Monterey Pass. Maxwell was promoted to captain on August 22, 1863.

83. Lt. Richard N. Vanatter of Co. M, 1st Michigan Cavalry, wounded in the fighting at the Monterey Pass.

84. Lt. Col. Ebenezer Gould of Owosso, wounded in action at Hagerstown on July 12.

85. Lt. Thomas J. Dean of Co. D, 5th Michigan Cavalry, wounded on the East Cavalry Field.

86. Capt. George N. Dutcher of Co. I, 5th Michigan Cavalry, wounded during the Battle of Hanover, June 30, 1863.

87. Lt. George W. Crawford of Co. F, 6th Michigan Cavalry, badly wounded during the fighting at Falling Waters on June 14, 1863. Crawford lost a leg as a consequence of his wound.

88. Lt. Edward W. Potter of Co. E, 6th Michigan Cavalry, wounded and captured at Falling Waters.

89. Lt. Seymour Shipman of Co. D, 6th Michigan Cavalry, wounded in the fighting at Hunterstown on July 2, 1863.

90. Lt. James G. Barney of Co. C, 7th Michigan Cavalry, wounded and captured in the fighting on East Cavalry Field. Barney escaped that same day and made his way back to his unit.

91. Lt. James L. Carpenter of Co. F, 7th Michigan Cavalry, also wounded and captured in the fighting on East Cavalry Field. Like Barney, Carpenter also escaped and made his way back to his unit. He was commissioned captain on July 8.

92. Lt. Elliott Gray of Co. B, 7th Michigan Cavalry, wounded in the fighting at Williamsport, Maryland on July 8, 1863.

93. Sgt. Caleb Griffith of Co. C, 7th Michigan Cavalry, wounded in the fighting at the Monterey Pass. Griffith was not commissioned as an officer until January 20, 1864.

94. Capt. Alexander Walker of Co. A, 7th Michigan Cavalry, wounded in the fighting on the East Cavalry Field.

The Michigan Cavalry Brigade in the Wilderness: A Paper Read Before the Michigan Commandery of the Loyal Legion

by Gen. Jas. H. Kidd (1889)

ON THE 27TH of May, 1864, the First Michigan Cavalry having, early in the morning, effected a crossing at Dabney's Ferry, on the Pamunkey River, General Custer ordered me, then in command of the Sixth Michigan, to take the road leading from Hanovertown and push on in advance toward Hanover Court House. We had gone but a mile or so when, in the midst of a dense wood, a force which proved to be dismounted cavalry was encountered, strongly posted behind earthworks which had been hastily thrown up for the purpose. The regiment was dismounted on the right of the road, and the First Michigan, following closely, went in on the left and the two regiments made a vigorous assault, but met with too stubborn a resistance to carry the works at once. A band in the rear of the enemy's line was playing "The Bonny Blue Flag," indicating the presence of a brigade at least in our front. Noticing that a portion of the enemy's fire came from far to the right, I sent the sergeant-major to the rear with word that my flank was in danger and that the line ought to be prolonged in that direction. The non-commissioned officer returned and reported that the message had been delivered to the brigade commander, but that it was overheard by the major-general commanding the division, "a pompous infantry officer but recently assigned to a cavalry command,"[1] whose arrogant bearing made him exceedingly unpopular with Buford's and Kilpatrick's veteran troopers, who had been accustomed to serve under men who could do harder fighting with less airs. This officer exclaimed with a good deal of impatience and undisguised contempt: "Who in h-ll is this who is talking

35

about being flanked?" I was mortified at this and resolved to never again, under any circumstances, admit to a superior officer that the idea of being flanked had any terrors for me, a resolution which was religiously adhered to so long as I was privileged to have a command in the field.

Custer, however, did not wait to strengthen his line in front, but, taking the other two regiments of his brigade (the Fifth and Seventh Michigan) made a detour by way of Hawes' Shop,[2] and came in on the flank of the force which the First and Sixth were ineffectually trying to dislodge from its strong position, and which held on tenaciously so long as it was subject to a front attack only. But as soon as Custer made his appearance on its flank, the enemy, a brigade of North Carolinians, under the rebel General Gordon,[3] abandoned the earthworks and fled precipitously, the First and Sixth promptly joining in the pursuit. Custer's approach was heralded by an amusing incident. The band that had been challenging us, with its lips of brass, close to the rear of Gordon's line, abruptly stopped in the midst of one of its most defiant strains, and the last note of "The Bonnie Blue Flag" had scarcely died on the air when far to our left and front were heard the cheery strains of "Yankee Doodle." No other signal was needed to tell of the whereabouts of our Michigan comrades and, in an instant, our line was rushing forward, only to see, as it emerged into the opening, the tarheels of the South making swift time toward Crump's Creek, closely followed by a mounted charge of Custer and his Michiganders. The latter had easily accomplished without loss, by the flanking process, what he had tried in vain to do with hard fighting and severe loss by the more direct method.

This incident is narrated to accentuate what follows:

The fear of being flanked was an ever present terror to the Army of the Potomac; and it was by no means confined to the battalion commanders, either. The apparition which appeared to McDowell at Manassas[4]; to Pope at the Second Bull Run[5]; to Hooker, at Chancellorsville,[6] flitted over the Wilderness, and was one of its causes, if not *the* cause, why that campaign was not successful.

There is no doubt, either, that General Meade[7] placed too low an estimate upon the value of cavalry as a factor in battle, and failed to appreciate the importance of the presence of Sheridan's troopers upon his left. If Meade and Hancock[8] had known Sheridan as they knew him a year later when he intercepted the flight of Lee's army at Five Forks and Sailor's Creek,[9] there would have been no nervous apprehension that Longstreet might re-enact in the Wilderness the part played at Chancellorsville by Stonewall Jackson.

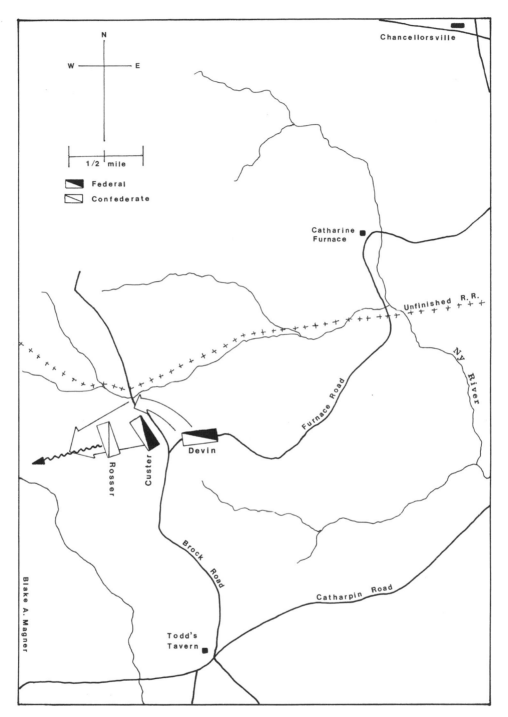

The Wilderness, May 6, 1864

"hard pressed." The Fifth Michigan and Seventeenth Pennsylvania, both under General R. A. Alger, then colonel of the Fifth Michigan, came at the same moment of time to the rescue of the Sixth Michigan.

General Sheridan's report gives a very meagre and inadequate account of the cavalry fight in the Wilderness. In his book, he dismisses it with a paragraph. That was to be expected. His corps was scattered over a wide area, its duty, to guard the left flank and all the trains, and he was not present in person when Custer put an abrupt stop to Hampton's impetuous advance. It is now known that Sheridan was hampered by interferences from army headquarters that his plans miscarried, and the relations between himself and his immediate superior that the doughty little warrior declared to General Meade that he would never give the Cavalry Corps another order. But, by General Grant's intervention, these difficulties were reconciled and Sheridan was soon off on his memorable raid, which resulted in the bloody battle of Yellow Tavern,[16] and the death of the foremost of the Confederate cavalry chieftains, General J.E.B. Stuart.[17]

The Michigan Cavalry Brigade (by which name it will be known in history), whose exploit in the Battle of the Wilderness it is the purpose of this paper to give, somewhat more in detail than it can be found in the official records, was organized early in the year 1863. It consisted at first of five regiments, viz: The First, Fifth, Sixth and Seventh Michigan, and First Vermont regiments[18] of volunteer cavalry. During the campaigns of that year it was known as the Second Brigade, Third Division, Cavalry Corps. General Judson Kilpatrick was the division commander, and George A. Custer had the Second Brigade. It was his first command, and one which he assumed on the battlefield of Hanover, Pennsylvania, during the Gettysburg Campaign, June 30, 1863. Previous to that he had been a subaltern on the staff and in the United States regular cavalry. Though his rise in rank was so rapid, he leaped at once to the front rank of the generals of brigade, and became the idol, as well as the ideal, of his men. There are those who think that the prestige which the Michigan brigade attained in the Potomac cavalry was due, in great part, to the genius of its commander. Such a judgment, however, does injustice to the officers and men who served under him, who are justly entitled to a share in the honors which fell to his lot.

When the cavalry corps was reorganized under Sheridan, the Michigan Brigade was transferred and became the First brigade, First division, the First Vermont, much to the regret of the brave Green Mountain boys, and of their Michigan comrades as well, remaining behind in the Third division, then commanded by General James H. Wilson.[19]

The regiments, taken by number, were commanded respectively by Lieut. Col. Peter Stagg,[20] Col. Russell A. Alger, Maj. James H. Kidd and Maj. Henry W. Granger.[21] Although the movement of the Army of the Potomac began May 3, it was the morning of May 4 when the Wolverine troopers left their camp near Culpeper and headed for Ely's Ford, on the Rapidan River. The Second and Third divisions had the honor of leading the advance, and preceded the infantry at the crossing the day before. At 3 o'clock on the morning of the 5th, the march was resumed, and crossing at Ely's Ford, the First division moved to Chancellorsville and was encamped that night at the Furnaces, south of the Orange plank road, about midway between Wilderness Church and Todd's Tavern, in the rear of the left of the Union line.

Early on the morning of the 6th "boots and saddles," and "to horse" summoned the brigade to arms, and at 2 o'clock A.M. it was on the march by the Furnace road towards its intersection with the Brock turnpike. Gregg was at Todd's Tavern, at the junction of the Catharpin and Brock roads. Custer was to be the connecting link between Gregg's division and Hancock's corps. Devin, with the Second brigade,[22] was ordered to report to Custer. Wilson had been out on the previous day on the Orange plank road and pike, where he encountered Stuart's cavalry, and was roughly handled. While moving up in the darkness towards the position at the cross-roads, we came upon the scattered troopers of the First Vermont, moving to the rear. They were greatly chagrined over their defeat of the day before, and declared that they did not belong to the Third division, but were the "Eighth Michigan." "Come along with us, boys," said their old Michigan friends. "I wish we could," they all replied. Wilson had Kilpatrick's fatuity for getting into scrapes, but lacked his skill in getting out.

Arriving at his destination before daylight, Custer posted his troops so as to be ready to meet the expected attack. Two squadrons,[23] one from the First Michigan, the other from the Sixth, commanded respectively by Capt. George R. Maxwell[24] and Capt. Manning D. Birge,[25] were sent out to picket the front on the Brock road. The line of battle was formed in the woods, facing a cleared space of open country, beyond which dense timber served as a screen to prevent the enemy's approach from being seen. The right was held by the First and Sixth Michigan, formed in two lines, regimental front, the Sixth in rear, the men standing "in place rest" in front of their horses. It was prolonged to the left by the Fifth and Seventh Michigan and Devin's brigade, composed of the Fourth, Sixth and Ninth New York, and Seventeenth Pennsylvania. Devin, however, did not arrive on the ground until the battle was well under way. The right of the line was "in the air," so far as was at that time known, the infantry not being in sight. The open or field directly in front, extended some 200 yards beyond our position to the right, and it was, perhaps, 500 yards across it to the woods. The timber, in which we formed, extended from the rear, clear around the right and across the front. In other words, the patch of open ground was surrounded, on three sides at least, by dense woods. The alignment faced in a westerly direction, and was back in the timber far enough to be hidden from an approaching foe. To the right of us, and as it turned out, somewhat to our rear, lay the Army of the Potomac, which had been battling with Lee all the previous day; and orders had been issued for the fighting to be resumed at 5 o'clock in the morning.

Thus we stood, prepared, in a state of expectancy, awaiting the sounds that were to summon us to battle.

The brigade band was posted near the left flank of the First Michigan.

General Custer, alert and wary, with a portion of his staff, was out inspecting the picket line.

The horse artillery had not yet arrived.

Every trooper was on the alert, ready for whatever might come.

The field, of which mention has been made, was bisected by a ravine, nearly diagonally from left to right, the ground sloping into it from front and rear. This ravine was to play a prominent part in the fight that ensued.

Suddenly the signal came. A picket shot was heard, then another, and another. Thicker and faster the spattering tones were borne to our ears from the woods in front. Then it was the rebel yell, at first faint, but swelling in volume as it approached. A brigade of cavalry,[26] led by the intrepid Rosser,[27] was charging full tilt towards our position. He did not stop to skirmish with the pickets, but, charging head-long, drove them pell-mell into the reserves, following closely at their heels, with intent to stampede the whole command.

It was a bold and brilliant dash, but doomed to fall short of complete success, for, "when Greek meets Greek then comes the tug of war."

Rosser had met his match.

When the rebel charge was sounded, Custer was near his picket line, and, scenting the first note of danger, turned his horse's head toward the place where he had hidden his Wolverines in ambush, and, bursting into view from the timber beyond the field, we saw him riding furiously in our direction. When he reached the edge of the woods, circling to the front as he rode, he bade the band to play, and, with sabre arm extended, shouted to the command, already in the saddle, "Forward, by divisions."

As the band struck up the inspiriting strains of "Yankee Doodle," the First Michigan broke by sub-divisions from the right, the Sixth following, and the two regiments charged with a yell through the thick underbrush out into the open ground, just as the rebel troopers emerged from the woods on the opposite side. Both commands kept on in full career until they reached the edge of the ravine, when they stopped, the rebels, apparently surprised by our sudden appearance and audacity, Custer well content with checking Rosser's vicious advance. Some of the foremost men kept on and crossed sabers in the middle of the ravine. One squadron of rebels, charging in column of fours, went past our flank, about one hundred yards to the right, and then, like the French army which marched up a hill, turned and charged back again, without attempting to turn their head of column towards the point where Custer was standing at bay, with his Michiganders clustered thick around him. Pretty soon the rebels ran a section of artillery into the field and opened on us with shell. Every attempt to break our lines failed however, the Spencer carbines proving too much of an obstacle to overcome.

The Fifth and Seventh Michigan were doing excellent service on the left, forging to the front and threatening the right of the rebel position. But it was evident our own right was vulnerable, and Custer ordered Major Kidd to take the Sixth, move by the rear to the woods on the right, dismount the men, and, as he expressed it, "Flank that battery." The regiment had become much scattered in the charge, but the rally was sounded and as many men as could be quickly gathered were withdrawn from the field, and, obeying the order with as much alacrity as possible, in a few minutes were in position and moving briskly forward through the thick woods. But they had not proceeded far when a strong force of dismounted cavalry was encountered. Both commanders seem to have ordered a simultaneous movement with a similar purpose, viz: to flank and attack the other's rear. The two forces met, very nearly on the prolongation of the line held by the mounted men of the First, Fifth and Seventh Michigan, east of the ravine. The rebel line extended beyond our right as far as we could see, and it was evident that we were outnumbered by at least three to one. But the little force stood bravely up to their work, using their Spencer carbines with deadly effect, and checking the advance of the enemy in their immediate front. Seeing that the left of the rebels were passing around us, the captain of the left company was directed to hold his position at all hazards. The right was swung back to protect our rear. At the same time an officer was dispatched to General Custer with an appeal for reinforcements.

The entire of the Second brigade was now up, and a battery, which arrived after the withdrawal of the Sixth, had been placed in position and opened on the enemy. The battle was still raging in the field, but General Custer sent the Fifth Michigan, Colonel Russell A. Alger commanding, and the Seventeenth Pennsylvania, Lieutenant Colonel J. Q. Anderson[28] commanding, to the relief of the Sixth. The reinforcements came none too soon. The rebels confident in their superior numbers, were pressing us hard. In a solid line of two ranks, with Spencer rifles full shotted, the two magnificent regiments deployed into position on our right. Then moving forward by a left half-wheel, the tables were turned on the too exultant foe, and he was forced gradually back. Close up to the line, cool as if on parade, rode the commander of the Fifth Michigan, Colonel Alger, now in command of the entire line. "Steady men, forward," he was heard to say; and with a responsive shout, the men swept on through the woods, driving everything before them. At the same time the mounted men of the First and Seventh charged the force in their front. The enemy gave way in disorder, was routed and fled, leaving his dead and wounded in our hands. His repulse was complete and crushing, and we saw nothing more of him that day. The Michigan brigade had won a signal victory, momentous in its consequences, for it saved the Union left from the disaster which was so much dreaded, the fear of which neutralized half of Hancock's command during the entire of that day. No one who witnessed it will ever forget the superb courage and conduct of General Alger and his command, when they swung into line on the right of the Sixth Michigan and instantly turned a threatened defeat into a magnificent victory.

In the mean time what was the infantry doing? After the repulse of Rosser it was found that there was a line of infantry not far to our right and rear. Attention was called to the fact when some of the cavalrymen who had been straggling in that direction returned and said that the Twenty-sixth Michigan infantry was a little way off, and a good many of the men went over for a brief hand-shake with friends therein.

Hancock was ready to advance, but learning that Longstreet was threatening his left flank, sent a division of infantry, commanded by Gen. Barlow, to cover the approaches by which Longstreet was expected.

Gen. Sheridan, (*Memoirs*, Vol. 1, pages 362–363)[34] says that:

On the Sixth, Gen. Meade became alarmed about his left flank and sent a dispatch saying: "Hancock has been heavily pressed and his left turned. You had better draw in your cavalry to protect the trains."

And again:

On the morning of the Sixth, Custer's and Devin's brigades had been severely engaged before I received the above note. They had been most successful in repulsing the enemy's attacks, and I felt that the line could be held. But the dispatch from Gen. Hancock was alarming, so I drew all the cavalry close in around Chancellorsville.

And:

The firing had hardly begun when Hancock was informed that the left wing was seriously threatened, so as to fully occupy Barlow. The enemy's dismounted cavalry opened on him with artillery and pressed forward their skirmish line. The rapid firing of Sheridan's attack helped to confirm the impression that this was a serious flank attack by the enemy. These repeated reports prevented Hancock from throwing his full strength into the attack along the plank road.

From these considerations it appears plain that the failure of Barlow and Gibbon to advance permitted Longstreet to swing in front of those two divisions and attack Birney's left, thus neutralizing Hancock's victory over Hill; whereas, if they had advanced as ordered, they would have struck Longstreet's flank and probably crushed it.

Second—The attack on Birney caused Sheridan's cavalry to be drawn in from a position they had successfully held against every assault; from which, indeed, they had driven the enemy's cavalry in head-long flight.

Third—This was the dismounted cavalry that attacked Barlow, and the only force that threatened him; the same with which the Michigan Brigade was contending in front of Barlow, and which was so handsomely repulsed by General Alger after his arrival with the reinforcements. The artillery was doubtless the same battery spoken of, which was run into the field at the time of Rosser's charge.

All of which demonstrates that in battle, as in the ordinary affairs of life, imaginary dangers often trouble us more than those which are real.

The Twenty-sixth Michigan was in Barlow's division. They had bee: interested listeners to, if not spectators of the cavalry fight. The conte: between the mounted men in the woods had been almost, if not quite j their front, and occasional shots had come their way.

Why did not Barlow, or, indeed, Gibbon's[29] entire command, move 1 at the time when the Sixth Michigan was contending alone with a superi force directly in its front?

The answer to that question is in the sealed book which contains 1 reason of Grant's failure in the Wilderness.

Let us see.

Grant's orders to corps commanders were to attack Lee's army at 5 A May 6.

Longstreet had not arrived, but was expected up in the morning, prisoners reported he would attack the Union left. Hancock was ord to look out for· his left. Barlow's division was posted for that purp Hancock's corps was divided into two wings, the right wing under Bii consisting of the three divisions of Birney, Mott[30] and Getty[31]; the left v of Gibbon's and Barlow's divisions under Gibbon. Barlow, as has been : was to look after the extreme left. Wright and Warren attacked Ew the hour, but were unsuccessful. Hancock's assault upon Hill was pletely unsuccessful. But Longstreet arrived in the nick of time to save But Hancock's attack was with Birney's command, and when Long arrived he struck the left flank of Birney. Where were the two divisi Gibbon, posted for the very purpose of looking out for Longstreet.

In General A. A. Humphrey's *Virginia Campaigns,*[32] page 40, w

At 7 A.M. General Hancock sent a staff officer to General G informing him of the success of his right wing, and directing] attack the enemy's right with Barlow's division. This order . . . w partially obeyed. Had Barlow's division advanced as directed, he eral Hancock) felt confident that the enemy's force would hav defeated. The case of his failure was probably owing to the ei approach of Longstreet on his (Barlow's) left.

Again:

At 8.50 A.M. Hancock began an attack, with Birney's wi Gibbon's division of the left wing.

Gen. Grant, in his *Memoirs*[33] (pp. 196–197):

Notes

1. Kidd refers to Brig. Gen. Alfred Thomas Archimedes Torbert, a Delaware-born West Pointer. For the first two years of the war, Torbert commanded infantry in the Army of the Potomac. He commanded a brigade of infantry during the spring and summer of 1863 and was a competent if unspectacular commander. In April 1864, as part of the reorganization of the Army of the Potomac's Cavalry Corps, Torbert was assigned to command of the First Cavalry Division, formerly commanded by Brig. Gen. John Buford, who had died of typhoid fever in December 1863. Warner, *Generals in Blue*, 508–9. Kidd and Torbert had an intense personality conflict that led to Torbert's removing Kidd from command of the Michigan Cavalry Brigade in October 1864.

2. A brutal cavalry fight occurred at Haw's Shop on May 28, 1864. The Michigan Cavalry Brigade was heavily engaged there, rescuing Gregg's Division from imminent destruction at the hands of the Confederate cavalry.

3. Brig. Gen. James B. Gordon, commander of a brigade of North Carolina Cavalry. Gordon was mortally wounded at head of his troops.

4. Kidd refers to Maj. Gen. Irvin McDowell, commander of the Union forces at the First Battle of Bull Run in the summer of 1861, who was the subject of a successful flank attack by the Confederates that was the decisive blow of the battle.

5. Maj. Gen. John Pope's Army of Virginia was routed by a sledgehammer blow of a flank attack launched by Lt. Gen. James Longstreet's corps of the Army of Northern Virginia on the afternoon of August 30, 1862. The successful attack drove Pope's army from the field in a wild rout.

6. Maj. Gen. Joseph Hooker, commander of the Army of the Potomac, a huge and well-equipped army, was routed by a successful flank attack launched by the corps of Lt. Gen. Thomas J. "Stonewall" Jackson, which rolled up Hooker's flank.

7. Maj. Gen. George Gordon Meade, commander of the Army of the Potomac from June 28, 1863, until the end of the Civil War.

8. Maj. Gen. Winfield Scott Hancock, commander of the Army of the Potomac's Second Army Corps.

9. Critical actions fought on April 1 and April 6, 1865, forced the evacuation of the Confederate capitol at Richmond and were major factors in bringing about the surrender of the Army of Northern Virginia on April 9, 1865, at Appomattox Court House, Virginia.

10. Brig. Gen. Francis Channing Barlow, commander of a fine, veteran infantry division of the Army of the Potomac's Second Corps.

11. Lt. Gen. A. P. Hill, commander of the Army of Northern Virginia's Third Corps, was a member of the legendary West Point Class of 1846.

12. Lt. Gen. Richard S. Ewell, commander of the Army of Northern Virginia's Second Corps.

13. Fought on October 19, 1864, the Battle of Cedar Creek was the decisive engagement of the 1864 Shenandoah Valley campaign.

14. In May 1864 Merritt commanded the Reserve Brigade of the First Division of the Army of the Potomac's Cavalry Corps. Merritt later commanded the First Division and eventually assumed command of the Cavalry Corps. Merritt served in the U.S. Army for nearly forty years and was one of the finest soldiers of the nineteeth century.

15. *Century Magazine* commissioned a series of articles by the participants of the Civil War that were serialized in the magazine. Later, those articles were compiled and published as a set of four books. See Robert U. Johnson and Clarence C. Buel, eds., *Battles and Leaders of the Civil War*, 4 vols. (New York: Century Publishing Co., 1884–1904).

16. The Battle of Yellow Tavern was fought on May 9–10, 1864, not far from Richmond.

17. Stuart was mortally wounded in whirling melee on the first day of the Battle of Yellow Tavern, and he died several days later.

18. The 1st Vermont Cavalry, which was formerly a part of the 1st Brigade of the Third Cavalry Division, was assigned to the Michigan Cavalry Brigade during the winter of 1863–64. It soon became known as the "Eighth Michigan Cavalry."

19. Brig. Gen. James Harrison Wilson, West Point Class of 1860, was known as a favorite of Lt. Gen. Ulysses S. Grant. He had not commanded any large bodies of men prior to being assigned to command of the Third Cavalry Division. He and Custer were bitter rivals, and Custer despised Wilson. Custer was senior to Wilson in rank and should have been entitled to command of the Third Division upon Kilpatrick's relief in the spring of 1864. In order to ensure that Wilson got command of the Third Division, the Michigan Cavalry Brigade was transferred to the First Division. Wilson was be relieved of command of the Third Division in October 1864, and Custer was then promoted to command of the Third Division.

20. Lt. Col. Peter Stagg of the 1st Michigan Cavalry succeeded Kidd as commander of the Michigan Cavalry Brigade in the fall of 1864. Stagg and Kidd were rivals who did not get along well.

21. Maj. Henry W. Granger of Grand Rapids commanded the 7th Michigan Cavalry for a brief time. He was killed in action at Yellow Tavern on May 11.

22. Col. Thomas C. Devin of New York commanded the Second Brigade of the 1st Cavalry Division. Known alternately as "Old Warhorse" or "Buford's Hard Hitter," Devin was a superb horse soldier who eventually achieved the rank of major general of volunteers and colonel in the Regular Army after the Civil War.

23. Squadrons typically consisted of two companies of cavalry.

24. Capt. George R. Maxwell, of Custer's adopted home town of Monroe, Michigan, commanded Co. E of the 1st Michigan Cavalry. He was wounded in battle three times, including at Hawe's Shop on May 28, 1864. At Five Forks, on April 1, 1865, he would lose a leg to a terrible wound.

25. Capt. Manning D. Birge, of Grand Rapids, commanded Co. A of the 6th Michigan Cavalry.

26. One of the finest brigades of Confederate cavalry, this brigade was known as the Laurel Brigade. Made up entirely of troopers from the Shenandoah Valley, it consisted of the 7th, 11th, and 12th Regiments of Virginia Cavalry and the 35th Battalion of Virginia Cavalry.

27. Brig. Gen. Thomas L. Rosser of Virginia was also a member of the West Point Class of 1860. While there, he and Custer became close friends. They met in battle a number of times during the Civil War. Rosser was badly wounded by a trooper of the Michigan Cavalry Brigade on June 11, 1864.

28. Lt. Col. James Q. Anderson commanded the 17th Pennsylvania Cavalry. He was wounded and captured during the fighting in the Wilderness campaign and was liberated during Sheridan's Trevilian Raid during June 1864.

29. Brig. Gen. John Gibbon, a member of West Point's Class of 1847, was a fine soldier. During the Wilderness campaign, he commanded the Second Division of the Army of the Potomac's Second Army Corps.

30. Brig. Gen. Gershom Mott commanded the Fourth Division of the Army of the Potomac's Second Army Corps.

31. Brig. Gen. George W. Getty commanded the Second Division of the Army of the Potomac's Sixth Army Corps.

32. Andrew A. Humphreys, *The Virginia Campaign of '64 and '65* (New York: Charles Scribner's Sons, 1883).

33. Ulysses S. Grant, *The Personal Memoirs of U.S. Grant*, 2 vols. (New York: Charles L. Webster, 1885).

34. Philip H. Sheridan, *Personal Memoirs of P. H. Sheridan*, 2 vols. (New York: Charles L. Webster, 1888).

Charge of the First Cavalry Division at Winchester

by Gen. James H. Kidd

THE SERVICES RENDERED by our cavalry in the war for the suppression of
the rebellion have been generally acknowledged; yet many thrilling incidents have been suffered to go unrecorded, because unwitnessed by re-
porters for the public journals, and are treasured up only in the memory of
those who participated actively, and who, seldom quitting the saddle even
for a day, had little leisure to perform the duties of chronicler of events.

"Cavalry," said General Morgan of revolutionary notoriety,[1] "are in the
eyes of the infantry." But, in the late war, a cavalry corps constituted something more than a corps of observation. Frequently, the only purpose served
by the horses was that of rapid transportation from one point to another.
The surface of the country did not often permit a mounted engagement,
and the command most familiar to a cavalryman's ears, on going into action
was, "Prepare to fight on foot." In this manner, although carrying weapons
of shorter range, and frequently without support, our cavalry often were
pitted against infantry, and not unfrequently were employed to carry entrenched positions. Always in advance, or on the flanks of the infantry, often
absent for a week from a base, with no supplies save those gathered from the
enemy's country, the life of a cavalryman was a succession of perilous and
exciting adventures.

The operations of Sheridan's cavalry,[2] during the last year of the war,
were confined almost entirely to one State. During that period, every section of Virginia was visited with fire and sword; her fairest fields were

drenched with the blood of heroes—horse and horseman had slaked their thirst in every considerable stream in the State.

The incident about to be described occurred in the Valley of the Shenandoah, which, before the rebellion, was the "Eden of America," but at the war's termination, was a desolate waste, with scarcely a barn, store-house, mill or fence, to relieve the monotony of the scene.

Harper's Ferry and Staunton—its northern and southern termini—are connected by a magnificent pike[3] over which large armies and immense trains of artillery and army wagons passed in alternate advance and rapid flight, during four years of war, but could not ruin.

Along this road, through the small towns, strode Lee and Jackson in front of their legions, with head uncovered, while the rustic population—decrepit old men, women, and children—flocked to gaze upon the sturdy chieftains with an admiration amounting almost to adoration.

Over this same thoroughfare the discomfited Confederates hurried back from Antietam and Gettysburg, while every house along the route was converted into a hospital for the wounded.

By the side of this road, under the hospitable shade of a tree, or close by the stone wall on either side, sleeps many a brave soldier, never more to waken at war's alarms—the untitled heroes of the conflict which decided the national fate.

Never before, during all the war for the Union, was cavalry employed more effectively, nor on so grand a scale, as at the battle of Winchester, which occurred on the 19th of September, 1864.[4] Let us briefly recall some of the incidents of that terrible engagement, which resulted in a disastrous defeat to Early,[5] but left 4,000 of our dead and wounded on the field.

Long before daybreak the reveille had sounded in the Union camps in the vicinity of Summit Point, and after a meal hastily dispatched, Sheridan's entire army was put in motion—Winchester being the objective point. At daybreak, Sheridan having crossed the Opequon river,[6] engaged Early with three corps of infantry (Sixth, Eighth, and Nineteenth). Wilson[7] was sent to operate with his division of cavalry, on the left flank, while Averel's[8] guns could be heard, indicating his approach from the north.—The first cavalry division was held in reserve, and drawn up in column of brigades, on the heights to the eastward of and overlooking Bunker Hill, the men being ordered to dismount and "stand to horse." During this interval of temporary inactivity, a word concerning the commander, and the composition of the

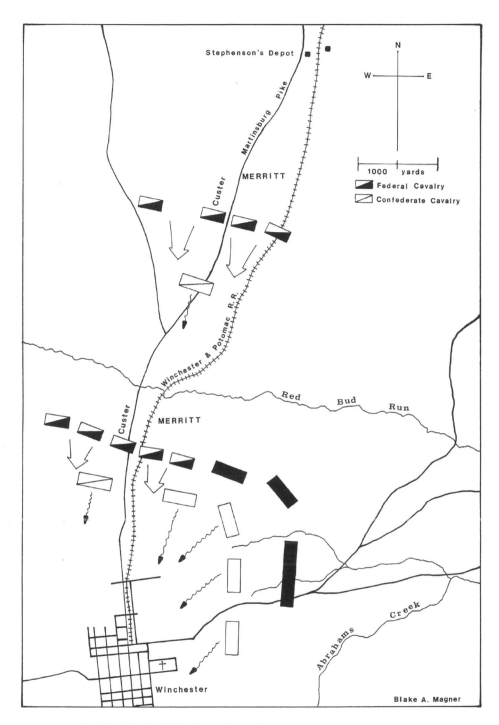

The Third Battle of Winchester, September 10, 1864

division, may not be inappropriate. Gen. Merritt, at the commencement of
the war, held I believe, the rank of captain in one of the regiments of United
States cavalry. Shortly afterward, upon recommendation of Maj. Gen.
Pleasonton,[9] he was commissioned Brigadier General of volunteers, and
before the close of the war was advanced to the grade of Major General of
volunteers. During the many hotly contested cavalry engagements, from
Upperville and Aldie[10] to Five Forks,[11] he was not accustomed to view the
progress of the battle from a distance, but plunged into the melee, encouraging his men by actual presence, and would not hesitate to place himself at
the head of a single squadron for a charge, even when commanding a division. By his coolness and intrepidity of action, he won for himself an envi-
able reputation, and enjoyed in a high degree the confidence of General
Sheridan.

Of the three brigades composing the first cavalry division, the first was
composed entirely of Michigan troops, armed with the Spencer carbine,
and commanded at that time, by the gallant Custer, late Major General of
volunteers. The records of the provost-marshal's office tell what service
has been performed by those hardy sons of the West under that dashing
officer. The Indiana brigade[12] was made up of the First New York Dragoons, the Fourth, Sixth, Ninth New York, and Seventeenth Pennsylvania cavalry. It commander, Colonel Devin, had been brevetted Brigadier
General of volunteers, a few days before, for gallantry at Front Royal.
This brigade bore its share of hard fighting, and has an honorable record.
Among the officers brevetted General, for distinguished services, should
be mentioned Colonel Alfred Gibbs,[13] and Lieutenant-Colonel Thomas J.
Thorp, of the First New York Dragoons,[14] and Colonel Chas. Fitzhugh of
the Sixth New York Cavalry. The third brigade was composed chiefly of
United States cavalry—men trained to the use of the saber from youth.[15]
It is a notable fact that the regular regiments of this brigade furnished a
large proportion of the generals officers of note in both the Union and
Confederate armies.—It had at the time under notice, as a re-enforce-
ment, detachments of the First Rhode Island, Second Massachusetts, and
Sixth Pennsylvania Cavalry; and was commanded by Colonel Lowell[16] of
the Second Massachusetts, who fell a month later in the memorable battle
of Cedar Creek.

During the long hours of morning the dismounted troopers reclined
on the ground in front of their horses, gaily chatting and smoking, or
cooking coffee, giving little heed to the ever-increasing roar of artillery

and rattle of musketry, which, though it could not intimidate, too plainly indicated the desperate nature of the conflict. The sun had reached the meridian, and still the din of battle did not recede. At 3 P.M., the situation was not materially improved. Though our infantry fought with the utmost heroism, every inch of ground was so stubbornly contested by the enemy that even our wounded could not be removed. A Southern journal, commenting on the battle at this stage, observed:"Our army had, up to this time, successfully resisted the onset of the Federal infantry, besides inflicting severe punishment; and would, without doubt, have been successful, had it not been for the cavalry—the flower of the Yankee army."[17]

At this critical moment, Merritt was ordered to charge with his whole division.—"To horse!" was sounded, and the Opequon was quickly left behind. As soon as the open country was gained, the command was rapidly deployed in line of battle. Fortunately, the conformation of the country was favorable to cavalry movements, for with the exception of a few ditches and dilapidated stone walls, there were no longer any obstructions. Steadily the line moved forward in the direction of Bunker Hill, with pace rapidly increased from a walk to a trot, from a trot to a gallop, while the formation was as carefully preserved as though the men were passing in review. The long line of horsemen, stretching across the plain from north to south, as far as the eye could reach, presented a magnificent spectacle, which, of itself, contributed wonderfully to inspiring the individual with that confidence which numbers always beget. In front of the line rode the division and brigade commanders, while battle-flags and guidons were gaily floating in the breeze, and bugles continually sounding the"advance."

Directly, above the clatter of the hoofs, and the jingling of scabbards, rang out the General's command, caught up and repeated by regimental squadron commanders—"*D-r-a-w sa-ber!*" It is difficult to conceive of the electrifying effect which this command, and its simultaneous execution, has upon the mind of the individual. Man and horse are suddenly wrought up to the highest pitch of excitement, while every instinct of self-preservation is absorbed and induced by riding at a pace continually accelerated, until it reaches its climax in the *charge*. A quarter of a mile in advance, Rosser, Lomax,[18] Imboden,[19] McCausland,[20] and Vaughan[21] were hurriedly forming for a counter charge.

As they made their appearance midway on the field, haughtily flaunting their colors, I heard an officer of ours remark to his men,"We shall soon witness the annihilation of the rebel cavalry," but, this was not to be;

for, after the first shock of battle, they disappeared from our sight as does the morning mist before the rising sun, nor halted until night and darkness had overtaken them many miles from Winchester.

As soon as the advancing column came within range, Early turned upon it his available artillery and shot and shell were rained almost continuously from redoubts on Bunker Hill, emptying many a saddle of its rider; but all the efforts of the Confederate commander to check the onset or break up the formation of the Federal cavalry were powerless. His own cavalry had ingloriously fled, and his artillery was also compelled to limber up and hastily decamp, to avoid capture, though not without the loss of several pieces, which were pounced upon by men of the regular and the Michigan brigades.

Now, the entire division hurled with irresistible force upon the left flank of the enemy. Then ensued a scene which language can but feebly portray, and which may well be called the carnival of death.

Suddenly, upon the vision of the Confederate infantry, flashed four thousand sabers, while the solid ground was shaken by the tread of the approaching column. I marvel exceedingly that then and there no effort was made to resist the charge by forming the hollow square, with its wall of bayonets, nor do I remember that it was resorted to under similar circumstances, during the war, although every regiment in either army was drilled in the evolution.[22]—A panic seized upon the opposing host; they left off harassing our tired Infantry, and, from a combative force, were quickly converted into a crowd of demoralized fugitives. The living mass surged backward, like waves driven before the wind.

To a foot-soldier the sight of hostile cavalry is always sufficiently appalling; and unless sheltered by breastworks, or, if the artillery fails to demoralize the horses and destroy the formation, he does not wait to be trampled under foot, but uniformly seeks safety in flight. On the part of Merritt's men, there was a feeling of supreme exultation; as rising in their stirrups, the rode straight at the doomed horde, dealing blows lustily about the head and ears of the devoted wretches.

Conspicuous in the charging body could be seen a tall officer (a returned prisoner of war), mounted on a handsome black charger, with the visor of his cap reversed, smarting under indignities endured while in captivity, wielding his saber remorselessly—the impersonation of a fiend. Under the excitement of the moment, the veriest coward was surprised into the performance of prodigious feats of valor. The gallant behavior of a soldier who hitherto had served in the humble capacity of cook, attracted observation. Encountering a Confederate colonel, punctilious about surrendering to a private soldier, he felled him to the earth by a well-directed blow which pierced his skull. A color-sergeant shared a similar fate at his hands. Scores of the Confederates threw themselves on the ground, and in piteous tones, sued for their lives. Some stood as if transfixed with terror, still grasping their muskets, while others skulked behind a friendly bush or stone to avoid being crushed. Here a single cavalryman might be seen hurrying to the rear a squad of prisoners, their eyes dilated with terror, their lips covered with foam from utter exhaustion; there a trooper proudly winning a Southern battle-flag—a trophy of his own prowess. In their anxiety to secure prisoners many of the men passed by these trophies, the capture of which is regarded as highly honorable. In this manner, the different regiments of the second brigade gathered up more by far than their own number.

A long score of wrong and injustice was on that day wiped out in blood; for, when the sun went down, not every saber, I ween, was sent home to its scabbard bloodless.—Only a few men were missing from my own regiment at night, and the bodies of these were found and buried on the most hotly contested field by those who followed after for that purpose. The rout of the enemy was signal and complete. As the whole Union army pushed on through Winchester in hot pursuit, the stripes and stars were exposed from many a window, while ladies waved their handkerchiefs from balconies in real or feigned congratulation.—Darkness alone interrupted the pursuit.

The ground over which the battle raged presented a sad spectacle of the horrors of war. Thousands of dead and wounded of either army were strewn about promiscuously, and a corps of surgeons and attendants laboring unremittingly for four days could not minister to all the sufferers before the wounds of some had become the habitation of loathsome worms. It is not my purpose, in confining this article to the first division, to detract from the dearly earned laurels of the other cavalry divisions, nor to ignore the hard fighting of our infantry, which was well attested by a long list of casualties.

In conclusion, we may add, that Early never recovered from the bitter defeat sustained at Winchester. His army was beaten in every subsequent engagement, until the remnant of it was captured by Sheridan's cavalry at Waynesboro,[23] the Southern General himself barely making his escape by a precipitate and solitary flight through one of the gaps of the Blue Ridge.

NOTES

1. Presumably, this refers to Brig. Gen. Daniel Morgan, who first commanded a regiment of riflemen in George Washington's Continental Army and who later gained fame as a guerrilla fighter. Morgan and his men took part in Benedict Arnold's unsuccessful assault on Montreal. Morgan's command played a major role in the defeat of Col. Banastre Tarleton's cavalry at the Battle of Cowpens in January 1781. A modern biographer described him as "Mighty of spirit, independent of mind, resourceful and self-reliant, a man who rose from humble immigrant stock to military fame, modest wealth, and national political office, Morgan symbolized Crevecoeur's image of the American—a wholly 'new' man." For a biographical sketch of Daniel Morgan, see Don Higginbotham, "Daniel Morgan: Guerrilla Fighter," in George Athan Billias, ed., *George Washington's Generals* (New York: William Morrow and Co., 1964), 291–316.

2. The makeup of the Cavalry Corps changed as a portion of the Army of the Potomac was sent into the Shenandoah Valley to pursue Lt. Gen. Jubal A. Early's Army of Virginia.

3. The Valley Pike, modern U.S. Route 11.

4. The September 1864 battle was actually the third battle of Winchester. The first was fought in May 1862; the second in June 1863, during the early phases of the Gettysburg campaign; and the third on September 19, 1864. Winchester, a strategic point, changed hands more than seventy times during the Civil War and was probably the most fought-over town of the war.

5. Lt. Gen. Jubal A. Early commanded the Confederate Army of the Valley in 1864.

6. The Opequon is actually a large creek, not a river.

7. Brig. Gen. James H. Wilson, commander of the Third Cavalry Division of Sheridan's Army of the Shenandoah.

8. Brig. Gen. William Woods Averell, whose independent division of cavalry became the Second Division of the Cavalry Corps of the Army of the Shenandoah in August 1864.

9. Maj. Gen. Alfred Pleasonton was the second commander of the Army of the Potomac's Cavalry Corps, leading it from May 1863 to April 1864. A competent administrator, Pleasonton deserves credit for molding the Cavalry Corps into a potent fighting force and for promoting Custer and Merritt to generals in June 1863.

10. The Battles of Aldie and Upperville were fought in the Loudoun Valley of Virginia on June 17 and 19, 1863, respectively. These brutal fights were important engagements, as Pleasonton's cavalry tried to find the Army of Northern Virginia as it advanced north into Pennsylvania. For more information on these fights, see Robert F. O'Neill, Jr., *The Cavalry Fights at Aldie, Middleburg and Upperville: Small but Important Riots* (Lynchburg, Va.: H. E. Howard Co., 1993).

11. The Battle of Five Forks, fought on April 1, 1865, was the key to Grant's breakout from the siege lines at Petersburg. Sheridan's victory at Five Forks opened Lee's flank to attack, ultimately leading to the evacuation of the lines at Petersburg and of the Confederate capitol at Richmond.

12. It is unclear why Kidd called this brigade the Indiana brigade, as there were no Indiana troopers in it. This was the Second Brigade, First Cavalry Division, commanded by Col. Thomas C. Devin of the 6th New York Cavalry.

13. Gibbs commanded the Reserve Brigade at one time and achieved the rank of brevet major general of volunteers. At war's end, he was appointed major of the newly formed 7th U.S. Cavalry.

14. Col. Thorpe was captured at the Battle of Trevilian Station on June 11, 1864.

15. The Reserve Brigade consisted of the 1st, 2d, and 5th U.S. Cavalry, as well as contingents of the 6th Pennsylvania and the 2d Massachusetts Cavalry.

16. Col. Charles Russell Lowell, a Harvard graduate who proved to be a gifted cavalry officer. By the fall of 1864, Lowell commanded the Reserve Brigade. He was mortally wounded in the Battle of Cedar Creek, October 19, 1864.

17. Unable to identify the source of this quote.

18. Maj. Gen. Lunsford Lomax, commander of a division of Confederate cavalry assigned to the defense of the Shenandoah Valley.

19. Brig. Gen. John D. Imboden, commander of a brigade of Confederate mounted infantry assigned to the defense of the Shenandoah Valley.

20. Brig. Gen. John McCausland, commander of a brigade of Confederate cavalry, was notorious for the burning of Chambersburg, Pennsylvania, earlier in the summer of 1864.

21. Brig. Gen. John C. Vaughn, also commander of a brigade of Confederate cavalry. Vaughn's brigade played a limited role in the fighting in the Shenandoah Valley.

22. Forming squares in echelon was a Napoleonic tactic designed for infantry in position to defend against mounted charges of cavalry. Briefly, the units would form hollow squares, facing outward, because horses will not charge into massed men and because the formation provides a 360-degree field of fire. There are a number of documented instances of this formation being used in combat in the Civil War, including on the first day of the Battle of Gettysburg. For more information on the use and formation of squares in echelon, see Baron Antoine Henri de Jomini, *The Art of War* (Philadelphia: J. B. Lippincott, 1862), 269–72.

23. On February 28, 1865, Custer's cavalry engaged the remnants of Early's shattered army on the hills surrounding Waynesborough, Virginia. The Yankee charge hit the Confederate flank and center at the same time, and Early's little force fled in a wild rout, with the commanding general lucky not to be captured by the Yankee juggernaut.

Memorial Address, Delivered in the Park at Ionia, May 30, 1885

by Gen. James H. Kidd

Mr. President, comrades of the Grand Army,[1] fellow soldiers and fellow citizens: It is a delicate and melancholy duty, a beautiful and touching custom, that calls us here to-day. For a moment to linger, and listen to such words as may be spoken, and then go forth, as in former years, in solemn and decorous procession to yonder hillside, there to deposit the floral gifts that mark our remembrance of those who have gone before, and our respect for their memory.

As time passes, the mind lingers more reverently over the memory of the dead, whose lives were laid upon the altar of their country. The events of those four awful years are fading away into the mists of the past. As we glance back through the vista of the intervening and rapidly receding years, the view becomes more and more indistinct. The war and its incidents pass in review before us, it is true, but they are vague phantoms—sober realities no longer. The rebellion has passed into history; it is an episode—a single scene—in the drama of the ages. The men who took part in it will soon be gone. A new generation has already come upon the stage. From Abraham Lincoln to Grover Cleveland seems but a span, but it is well-nigh a quarter of a century. The boy who was born on that dark day, when the loyal legions were swept back dismayed, defeated, across Bull Run, and on to Washington in panic and rout, is to-day older than were many of those who commanded regiments and brigades in the army of the union—older than were the great mass of those whose deeds, or whose heroic deaths, we are here met to commemorate; some of whose graves we will soon deck with vernal flowers, emblems of the beauty of their self-sacrifice, the fragrance of their example.

Perhaps, I am addressing to-day, not the scarred veteran only, bearing on his breast the badge of honorable service; the troops of the common-wealth sworn to do their duty, and emulous of the record of the soldiers of the grand army of the republic; the citizens upon the tablets of whose memory are engraven unfading recollections of the time when loyalty and treason were contending for the mastery in this land; the mother who has not ceased to mourn for her son; the lover whose cruel wound time will never heal; the widow and the fatherless, made such by the inexorable fatalities of that matchless struggle; but also young men and maidens, to whom the events of the rebellion are as a tale that is told—who know of Gettysburg and the Wilderness, of Chickamauga[2] and Cedar Creek, as they know of Blenheim[3] or Austerlitz,[4] or Palo Alto[5] or Yorktown.[6]

Each year the ranks of the young men are receiving recruits. Each year the ranks of the grand army are being decimated by death. Each year when the roll is called, fewer are left to answer to their names. It is but a span from that time to this, but another one as long, or a little longer, and the pale ashes of the last one of all that mighty host will have been returned to mother earth—of all that mighty host of patriots who went down into the sunny south to do or die for the cause they loved.

How swiftly are they going! Have you noted it? It is the irony of fate. They escaped death on many a hard-fought field, only to succumb to it at last. Thus hath it been in all ages and will be till the end of time. There is no escape from the inevitable. Where are the heroic defenders of Thermopylae, the Roman legions, Saladin and his Saracenic hosts, Richard the lion-hearted, Hannibal and Charlemagne? Where are Alexander, Caesar, Napoleon? And the myriads of lesser lights whose names have illumined the pages of the world's history?

And it is not alone the warriors who have gone to the land of shadows, for glancing back through the annals of the ages, we see a long, an endless procession of poets, philosophers, historians, prophets, statesmen, philanthropists; princes, potentates and peoples; the greatest, the wisest, the best of mankind, all alike, performing their brief part in the drama of life, and then passing over into the eternal silence of the unknown land.

The boast of heraldry, the pomp of power,
And all that beauty, all that wealth e'er gave.

A wait alike the inevitable hour.
The paths of glory lead but to the grave.

The thought of death causes a vein of melancholy to run through the human character, which gives it some of its most refined and ennobling graces. The man does not live who can look with complacency upon the somber surroundings of the tom, or think without a pang, of the narrow cell wherein he will one day be forever laid. The proudest, as well as the most humble cannot repress a desire that his last resting place may be a peaceful one, and that some decent respect may be paid to his remains. It is the instinctive protest of the human soul against the idea of destruction. He would fain have his mind diverted by some agreeable associations from the corruptions of the grave, where "the worm winds its cold coil" and the ghastly work of dissolution goes on. This yearning, is "the pleasing hope, the fond desire, the longing after immortality," of which Addison wrote. It has stirred the human imagination and given to poesy much of its pathos, and of its most thrilling imagery.

And what if, in the evening light
Betrothed lovers walk in sight
Of my low monument?
I would the lovely scene around
Might know no sadder sight nor sound.

I know, I know I should not see
The season's glorious show,
Nor would its brightness shine for me
Nor its wild music flow;

But if around my place of sleep
The friends I love should come to weep,
They might not haste to go.
Soft airs, and song, and light, and bloom,
Should keep them lingering by my tomb.

These to their softened hearts should bear
The thought of what has been,
And speak of one who cannot share

The brightness of the scene;
Whose part in all the pomp that fills
The circuit of the summer hills
Is—that his grave is green.
And deeply would their hearts rejoice
To hear again his living voice.

To do homage to the leaders of men, the few immortal names that are not born to die, art has taxed itself to the utmost, and song and "animated bust" have proclaimed their virtues and valorous deeds. But those more lowly, who are destined to obscurity, and who, "along the cool, sequestered vale of life, kept the noiseless tenor of their way," go to their rest relying on the spontaneous tributes of affection, which surviving friends may for a time bestow, to rescue their graves from neglect, and their names from oblivion.

The wave of patriotic fervor that swept over the land in 1861, stirred the heart of the nation to its depths and left a profound impress on the national character. But the patriotism of the hero, who cheerfully laid down his young life for the union, was scarcely more single-hearted, then the impulse of gratitude that led the great body of the people to look upon the survivors of that war as the wards of the government, and prompted Congress to grant them such liberal pensions as became a great and generous nation, saved by their efforts. I congratulate the soldiers whose lines have fallen in the pleasant places of the peninsular state, that the legislature has become infected with the same spirit. The time is coming—is now—when the members of the grand army of the republic need have no fear of the almshouse. Should misfortune, disease or poverty come upon you in your old age, Michigan will provide you with a home, where you may go with no sense of humiliation, dependence, or wounded pride, to pass your declining days. No morose or desponding feelings need assail you, should fortune take you there, but rather a feeling of satisfied contentment, for it is yours. You earned it. Enter thou, into thy reward.

And it was a profound sense of gratitude toward those who returned not, but poured out their life-blood to enrich the soil of their native land, that caused a revival of the elegant and touching custom of planting flowers on the graves of deceased soldiers, and made it national—giving to it, in a sense, the sanction and prestige of law, and appointing a suitable day for its observance.

Thus it is, that we come with simple and unaffected hearts, to pay the annual tribute of our admiration and gratitude. Yours be it, to bring the votive offering of vernal bloom; to weave garlands of fragrant flowers with which to decorate the habitations of the dead; to fleck the verdant sod beneath which they rest, with the lowly daisy and many a snow white emblem; to plant near by the eglantine and sweet-scented shrub, that the summer air may be filled with aromatic odors, as of perfumes wafted from the elysian fields that lie beyond the "the portal which we call death"; mine, to utter the few words, which if they be not like "pictures of silver" "fitly spoken," shall be, at least, heartfelt. Nor go with pomp, and idle ceremonial and garish parade, but in simple-hearted earnestness and,

> With a feeling of sadness and longing
> That is not akin to pain,
> And resembles sorrow only
> As the mist resembles the rain.

So from our sombre musings, turn we to brighter themes. There is no cloud which hath not a silver lining; and as we tenderly mournfully, perform these refining offices of affection, a gleam of sunshine comes athwart the gloom, and:

"There is no death; what seems so is transition."

Not to the inanimate clay, the mouldering heap of bones, the grinning skull—those hideous emblems of mortality—do we pay these tributes; but to that immortal part that will never die. May we not fondly hope that these departed heroes and friends are to-day—even now—looking on from a new life infinitely more glorious than the transitory and fugitive existence wherein they acted so well their parts?

Thus are departed heroes destined to a dual immortality; for while they like the flower that strikes its fibres in the corruptions of earth only to come forth in new splendor, have risen to realms of light, the recollection of their courage and patriotism; their splendid devotion and self-sacrifice, will never fade, so long as valor and virtue are valued as shining traits in human character.

The war of the rebellion was one of those great crises in human affairs which had to be. It was foreseen, but could not be prevented. Daniel Webster, sagacious beyond any other statesman of his time—Cassandra-like, uttered his prophecies to unbelieving ears. Secession, he said, meant war. There could be no peaceable withdrawal of states. But the cement that bound the union had become like wax. The heats engendered in a presidential election melted it as the mountain snow is melted by the morning sun. The secession of a state was the signal for war. It came. The prophecy was fulfilled. The people were blind to the danger. When the storm burst, it found them unprepared. For a moment the loyalty of the north was stunned, stupefied by the shock. In the south, many minds wavered and for a time hung in the balances hesitating between right and wrong; loyalty and treason; duty to the nation and a sentimental attachment to a state. Officers of the army and navy, senators, members of Congress, cabinet ministers, sworn to defend the government, finally deserted it, and for years sought to destroy the glorious stars and stripes, and set up a foul and treasonable standard in its place. But there were others, eternal honor and glory to their names, who could be seduced by no subtleties of reasoning to betray their country. "Grand old Pap Thomas"[7] was a noble type of the hero who knows no guide of conduct but inflexible adherence to the right. A Virginian by birth and in feelings, he remained true to his colors to the end.

War was inevitable, but war has its uses. Far be it from my purpose to palliate the horrors of war. It is a terrible thing—a better panacea for human ills, but a panacea still. As there are for the individual worse things than death, so there are for peoples things worse than war. Strange and paradoxical as it might seem, the advancement of the human race in civilization, in the arts, in learning, in all the ameliorating influences of civilized human intercourse, has been aided, if not in some degree brought about by the sword. The Greek conquests carried Grecian refinement along with them. The Roman legions taught the principles of rugged Roman virtue and valor to all the nations, and it was when sensuality and vice succeeded to the warlike spirit of the earlier times, that the Roman empire fell, a victim to its own effeminacy, overrun by the hordes of northern barbarians who had taken lessons in courage from their conquerors. But the Roman conquests had the effect to spread throughout the world the Latin language and literature, the borrowed erudition of Greece and the sturdy principles of primitive Roman character, so that the influence is felt even unto this day. Mahomet,[8] with the sword of Islam, came upon the scene when learning was about expiring in Europe, and for six centuries he and his successors kept it alive. From the arid wastes of Arabia to the sunny plains of Andalusia; from Baghdad to Cordova, all along the Mediterranean Sea, establishing universities which preserved the accumulated knowledge of the centuries until the revival of learning in Europe enabled the work to go on without their aid. The wars of the crusades brought about international intercourse and commercial prosperity. The revolt of the barons gave us *magna carta*; the English revolution—parliamentary privilege; the French and American revolutions—liberty. The thirty years war gave Europe religious toleration and erected a barrier against imperial absolutism. But for the French and English conquests in the New World, the red Indians of North America might yet be torturing and scalping each other by the banks of the Hudson and Delaware.

War has had much to do with developing national character. Napoleon's campaigns changed the ferocity of the revolution into the heroism of Marengo and Waterloo. The Anglo-Saxon, the highest type yet produced, is the result of the miscegenation of the races, brought about by war. It cost much bloodshed to blend the white and red roses, and it took four years to demonstrate that one southern man could not whip five Yankees.

What war had done for national, it has done for individual character. In the Roman tongue, the same word stood for virtue and for valor. To be virtuous was to be brave. In the broadest sense this is true. To be brave is to have the courage of your convictions; to dare to do right; knowing your rights to maintain them—to fight; to *die* for them if need be. "Fear not death; fear dishonor," was the injunction which the grandmaster gave the medieval knight, who had just taken the oath binding him to the profession of arms. The military school is a nursery of all the manly graces. The education of the true soldier teaches him to be brave, true, knightly, virtuous, and to hold his life lightly in the scale as against the honor of his country or his own integrity. Such teaching—the teaching of wars waged for a principle—in a good cause—is what makes men of real worth; the kind of men who prefer death to dishonor.

The war of the rebellion was a wicked war; and never had men a holier cause than did you, who went out under the starry banner to fight for the integrity of the Union.

The stupor was short-lived. The flash of a rebel gun against a federal fort fired the languid blood of a loyal-hearted people, and then was the mightiest uprising known to history. It was as unexampled as it was unexpected. Northern men had been bred to the arts of peace. From the close of the Revolutionary War the manhood of the nation had been put to no severe proof. The War of 1812 was of brief duration, and the affair with Mexico was carried on by a handful of regulars, assisted by a few volunteer regiments, mostly from the southern states. It required a violent stretching of even the youthful imagination to excite much military enthusiasm over the conquest of Mexico. The most picturesque figures on our side were Capt. May[9] and Colonel Harney,[10] neither of whom cut any particular figure afterwards. It was thought that commerce and the lust for grain, had quenched the martial spirit; that the blood of Ethan Allen,[11] and Putnam[12] and Stark[13] had so thickened in the veins of their descendants, that they would not fight; that the heroism displayed a hundred years ago by the Green Mountain Boys, and the soldiers of Breed's Hill[14] and Valley Forge was a thing of the past. The militia system had become unpopular and had been derided out of existence. The inherent valor, fortitude and fidelity that resided in the breasts of the men north of Mason and Dixon's line was not suspected even by the possessors of those traits. Men knew as little of the metal they were destined to display, as of the nature and magnitude of the task assigned them. Mr. Seward[15] said it would take ninety days; President Andrew D. White[16] thought it would last thirty years, and until another Gustavus Adolphus[17] appeared to throttle the slave power. Ellsworth,[18] the young Chicago tactician, was sent to New York City to raise a regiment of roughs, in obedience to the then popular delusion that bruisers were the best fighting material. But the hour came when the sleeping giant, unconscious of his strength, was aroused. All illusions were dispelled. The truth finally dawned, and then the outpouring came. It was sudden, spontaneous and widespread. It was confined neither to a sect nor to a party—hardly to a section—for there were loyal men even in the south. There was loyalty everywhere. What a spectacle was that, my comrades! So grand, so sublime, it seems like the work of inspiration. Ah! How well do you remember it! How your hearts throb; the blood bounds, and the eye flashes at the recollection! How proud of the part you took in it, however humble. Thrice happy those, who lived in that day, to not only see it, but to be in it, and of it—even a single drop in that great sea of patriotism.

From first to last twenty six hundred thousand men were enrolled on the side of the Union. More than a quarter of a million of these sealed with their lives their fidelity to the cause. This does not include those who have died since the close of hostilities from wounds or disease contracted in the service. Only one in twenty six was a drafted man or a substitute. The rest were volunteers. For the most part young men, they came from all walks of life. The pale-faced student left his Homer and Thucydides, to help make the materials for a new epic grander than the Iliad. The merchant exchanged the yard-stick for the musket. The book-keeper abandoned his desk for the drill-ground. The editor gives up the pen for the sword. The teacher parted with his pupils; the preacher with his charge. The farmer went from his half-turned furrow, the mechanic from his bench. Doctors dropped their pill-bags and lawyers their briefs. Mothers urged their sons into the ranks, and wives their husbands, with a fervent blessing and a prayer for their safe return. Young boys wept if refused the privilege of going into the ranks as drummer boys, if not bearing arms. The purest and loftiest motives animated them. Love of country was their inspiration. Most of them had not the incentive of rank and hope of preferment, but were common soldiers, privates in the ranks, receiving a paltry stipend as their recompense for risking life and limb; for braving disease, enduring hardships, severing the ties of home, relinquishing life-plans and ambitions. The green earth never resounded to the treat of a more intelligent, a braver or more heroic army of patriots than were the volunteers of 1861.

The story has been often told. The history of the next four years is familiar to you all. Those scenes in which you were actors are photographed on your memories. Even in your dreams you are often startled at the bugle blast "To Horse," hurrying into ranks at the ominous sound of the long roll; with set teeth climbing the frowning heights of Fredericksburg, or facing belching cannon before Atlanta. It may be at times the visions are more pleasing, and you revel amid the good thing of the smiling valley of the Shenandoah, or mingle joy with sorrow in the swelling song of "Sherman marching through Georgia." I need not dwell upon the record of those volunteers. I shall not recount what they did, nor follow them through their four years of warfare. I shall not describe their battles, their skirmishes, their midnight marches or long raids into the enemy's country for days and nights without rest or food—oftentimes marching by night and fighting by day for weary weeks together. I shall not relate how the panic-stricken mobs of Bull Run and Pittsburg Landing[19] were gradually transformed into the splendid armies of veterans, who faced death without flinching at Vicksburg and Cold Harbor[20]; how they fell by thousands with their faces to the foe; how they perished in northern hospitals and rotted in southern prison pens; how they were maimed for life by bullet and shrieking shell; how they charged with Sheridan and Custer in the Valley, with Hancock at Spottsylvania, with Hooker among the clouds[21]; how they stood, a wall of fire with McClellan at Malvern Hill,[22] with Thomas at Chickamauga, with Grant in the Wilderness; how they displayed

Spartan fortitude and Roman courage on a hundred battle-fields, and then, how, after the grand review, their work ended, the rebellion crushed, the Union saved, the great army of Grant, and the great army of Sherman, instead of seeking new worlds to conquer, folded their tents, and silently peacefully, without protest or murmur, melted away into the ranks of citizenship, to be soldiers no longer.

Oh! Volunteer of '61! For thy unselfish patriotism, fervent love of country, noble self-sacrifice; for courage, for endurance, for chivalric heroism, thy place is almost unique in history. Doubt did not deter, nor defeat dismay thee. When the cause seemed doomed, you faltered not. Did imbecility lead you to useless slaughter, you repined not, but with fortitude and faith pressed on to victory. In the presence of thy memory, I stand mute with admiration. The heart which is unmoved by thy deeds is dead to every noble impulse; the nation which does not acknowledge such devotion and fidelity is unworthy to be served by heroes. The simple tale of thy su±erings is the highest tribute that can be paid to thy memory. The history of thy generous self-sacrifice is thy loftiest eulogium.

Comrades: The great lesson to be learned from the war is the lesson of loyalty,—loyalty to our country, loyalty to our own manhood; loyalty to the better impulses within the heart which engender scorn of every mean and dishonorable act; loyalty to ourselves. And so may we order our lives as to lift them above all the sordid temptations of the world to the plane of high principle where stood the volunteer of '61. Thus may we be led into the elysian fields of prefect contentment and self-respect. For those who died in their country's cause we need not waste time in idle lamentation. They are indeed fortunate, for

> To every man upon this earth
> Death cometh soon or late;
> And how can man die better
> Than facing fearful odds
> For the ashes of his fathers
> And the temples of his gods.

NOTES

1. Kidd refers to a gathering of the Grand Army of the Republic, the principal Union veterans' organization.

2. A major Western Theater engagement, the Battle of Chickamauga was fought on September 19–20, 1863, just south of the Tennessee-Georgia border, a few miles from Chattanooga.

3. This was a major battle between French and allied forces, commanded by the Duke of Marlborough and fought on August 13, 1704, near the village of Blenheim, Austria. This battle was memorable as a result of the completeness of Marlborough's victory over the French forces and because it showed that divided command among allied armies could succeed.

4. Fought on December 2, 1805, the Battle of Austerlitz pitted French forces commanded by Napoleon Bonaparte against the allied forces of Austria and Russia. Notable for the crushing flank attack that routed the allied armies, Austerlitz was a brilliant victory for Napoleon's armies.

5. Part of Gen. Zachary Taylor's campaign in northern Mexico, the Battle of Palo Alto was fought on May 8, 1846. Arguably an American victory, Taylor's army allowed its Mexican adversary to escape intact.

6. The Siege of Yorktown was the decisive campaign of the American Revolution. The American army, commanded by Gen. George Washington and supported by both French infantry and the French navy, brought the British army of Lord Charles Cornwallis to bay on the narrow peninsula at Yorktown, Virginia. After a siege of three weeks, Cornwallis surrendered his army, effectively ending fighting in the American Revolution.

7. Maj. Gen. George H. Thomas, a Virginian who stayed loyal during war, is generally considered to be one of the key figures of the Civil War. Thomas, who commanded Union forces in Tennessee in the fall of 1864, crushed the remnants of the Confederate Army of Tennessee at the Battle of Nashville, fought on November 16, 1864. Known to his men as either "Old Pap" or "Old Slow Trot," Thomas was enormously popular with the men who served under him. He was one of the army commanders directly responsible for the Union victory.

8. This is Mohammed, founder of Islam.

9. Capt. Charles A. May of Washington, D.C., was a dragoon officer who distinguished himself in battle numerous times during the Mexican War.

10. Col. William S. Harney, another legendary dragoon, was one of four general officers in the U.S. Army at the outbreak of the Civil War. He was a Southern sympathizer and was unceremoniously removed from command early in the war as a result of an agreement that he made with Confederate general Sterling Price not to molest Price's Missouri State Guard so long as it committed no overt acts against the U.S. government. Harney retired in 1863 but was breveted major general at the end of the Civil War.

11. Gen. Ethan Allen of Vermont, commander of the Green Mountain Boys, one of the most famous fighting units of Washington's Continental Army.

12. Gen. Israel Putnam, another of Washington's principal subordinates, while politically astute, was not competent to command large forces. Putnam's poor dispositions led to Washington's defeat in the Battle of Brooklyn Heights.

13. Brig. Gen. John Stark of New Hampshire, commander of the victorious American forces at the Battle of Bennington, Vermont, fought in 1777. Stark's brother fought for the British and was killed in the Battle of Long Island.

14. Kidd refers to the 1775 battle known to history as the Battle of Bunker Hill, which was misnamed. This fight actually occurred on Breed's Hill.

15. President Lincoln's secretary of state, William Seward.

16. Chancellor of the University of Michigan at the outbreak of the Civil War.

17. King Gustavus Adolphus II, warrior king of Sweden, 1594–1632, was a brilliant general who was gifted in both strategy and tactics.

18. Col. Elmer Ellsworth, commander of a famed New York Zouave regiment, was killed by a Virginia secessionist in Alexandria in 1861. He was instantly made a martyr for the Union cause.

19. Also known as the Battle of Shiloh, fought on April 5–6, 1862.

20. The brutal and bloody battle at Cold Harbor, Virginia, fought at the beginning of June 1864. Ulysses S. Grant once wrote that the only order he ever regretted giving was for the second assault at Cold Harbor, an attack that cost the Army of the Potomac seven thousand casualties in less than fifteen minutes.

21. The Battle of Lookout Mountain, Tennessee, fought in November 1863, was known as the Battle among the Clouds, as a result of fog that socked in the top of Lookout Mountain during the fighting.

22. The Battle of Malvern Hill, the closing engagement of Maj. Gen. George B. McClellan's Peninsula campaign, was fought in June 1862.

Historical Sketch of General Custer

by James H. Kidd

To WRITE AN APPRECIATIVE and just account of the life and military services of General Custer is a task that would tax the resources of the most
gifted writer or student. To do even scant justice to the theme is more than
the author of this brief sketch may hope to accomplish. If, to the chance
reader, his effort shall appear to be rather the plea of an advocate or the
tribute of a friend, than the cold, dispassionate narrative of the historical
annalist, it will be the fault of the point of view of the critic; and it will not
be due to any want of historical accuracy on the part of the reviewer.

"Time at length sets all things even" and the sunlight of time, shining
through the mists of the years, at last, we venture to hope, has cleared
away the clouds of doubt, not to say distrust—some of them the manifes-
tation of misinformation, some of malevolence—which for many years
after his death obscured his fame.

Scarce forty years have passed—but a span, as time is measured on the
dial-plate of history—and how plain those things appear that then were
seen as "through a glass darkly."[1] His figure, from thus time on, will stand
out on the page of history, distinct as a piece of sculpture on the façade of
the temple of art; flawless as the noble equestrian statue erected to sym-
bolize his heroism and his virtues. The glamour of poetry, the winged
word of the orator, the affluent thought and lucid diction of the historian,
must all needs be at their best to adequately portray his genius as a solder,
his noble and lovable qualities as a man. In the language of an army officer,

who is also a competent military critic*—too high minded and generous to be warped by prejudice or professional jealousy—General Custer as a cavalry officer was "in a class by himself."

No higher tribute can be paid. It fully justifies the opinion often expressed by the writer that George Armstrong Custer was the foremost cavalry officer of his time, not expecting any, Federal or Confederate. His fame is the common heritage of all patriots of the reunited republic, and deserves to be jealously treasured and perpetuated. His last battle, notwithstanding all that has been said about it, was the crowning glory of a life full of exploits; for it marked him as an officer who, at the end as he had been at the beginning, was wholly devoted to his duty; who never hesitated in his obedience to orders, even when such obedience led, as it did, to inevitable death.

He was a man, take him for all in all, "whose like we shall not see again," a veritable Chevalier Bayard, absolutely "without fear and without reproach;" like Sir Philip Sidney, a gentleman and a knight whose accomplishments were many and who was an ornament to the profession of arms of which he was a most consummate master.

In the final analysis, we may truthfully say of him that what Seydlitz was to Frederick the Great; what Prince Rupert[2] was to Charles Stuart; what Joachim Murat[3] was to Napoleon Bonaparte; what James E. B. Stuart was to Robert E. Lee[4]; what Sheridan himself was to Ulysses S. Grant; such was Custer to Philip H. Sheridan; his right arm in battle, an ever present help in trouble. This his loyal friends have maintained always; this much his rivals now concede. Even in the regular army, the truth has prevailed. Rivalry has ceased to decry; envy no longer detracts. The impartial historian will place him in the temple of fame in the niche where he by right belongs, and in the acclaim no voices will join more heartily than those of the officers of the United States Army. They will point with pride to his record, which will animate them to the full measure of their duty, as that of a soldier who was the type of all that an American cavalry officer should be or can be.

George Armstrong Custer was born December 5, 1839. He died June 25, 1876. His birthplace was New Rumley, Ohio, near the Pennsylvania line. The scene where his death befell was in far away Montana, by the banks of the "Greasy Grass," the Indian name for the Little Big Horn

---

*General T. F. Rodenbough, brigadier general, U.S. Army, retired, secretary military service institution, Governor's Island, N.Y., editor of the *Journal*, formerly commanding Second U.S. Cavalry, Reserve Brigade, First Division, Cavalry Corps, Army of the Potomac.

River. His ashes rest at West Point on the Hudson, the site of the military school where he was taught the art of war and trained in the profession of arms; and where so many officers were educated who brought distinction to the name of the American soldier.

His origin was humble. The place where he first saw the light is so obscure as hardly to merit mention on the map. His father was a blacksmith who left the shop in Pennsylvania to become a small farmer in Ohio, and brought his forge with him. His ancestry, on his father's side, is traced back to Maryland, and to colonial times, but there is good reason to take with a grain of salt the statement of one of his biographers that his great grandfather was an officer of King George the Third's Hessian mercenaries.[5] He may have been of German descent, but the strain of martial blood that ran in the veins of himself and his brother "Tom,"[6] is suggestive of the fiery Celt or the mercurial Frank rather than of the phlegmatic Teuton.

His mother was his father's second wife and a widow when she married him. General Custer was the eldest of the children born to the union of Emmanuel Custer and the widow Kirkpatrick.[7] These parents, though poor, came of sturdy and self-reliant stock; were well-principled and fond of their children. His education was the best that the schools of the section afforded. That he made the best use of his opportunities is quite certain. His alertness of mind and vigor of body enabled him to be easily a leader among the boys his age, both in his studies and in athletics. With a wiry frame, a strong constitution, and perfect health, he was a natural leader of boys as in after years he became a leader of men. He was born to leadership.

From the time he was ten years of age until he was sixteen Custer lived alternately in New Rumley and in Monroe, Michigan. His parents remained on the old farm, but a half-sister, who had married a man named Reed[8] from Monroe went there to live and took her young brother with her.[9] The associations and educational advantages of that historical old town were of great benefit to him. He worked on his father's farm summers, attended school in Monroe winters, did what many noted men have done, earned his first money by teaching school.

Armstrong Custer was not a plodding student, but quick to learn. His brother, Nevin,[10] relates that he used to lie in the furrow and study during the noon hour when others were resting. There is no doubt that he was ambitious and dreamed dreams, as other bright boys have done. His father was a militia officer, and the story of the martial exploits of the United States Army in Mexico—of Palo Alto, of Cerro Gordo and Chapultepec—

inflamed the imagination of the youthful student and filled him with the desire to emulate their heroic deeds. He seems to have had an inspiration, sort of a prophetic intuition, that led him to make application for a cadetship at West Point. That was in 1856, when he was but sixteen years old. It was the year that the Republican Party presented its first ticket—Fremont and Dayton—for president and vice president. John A. Bingham had been chosen to Congress as a Republican in 1854, from the district in which New Rumley was situated. He was re-elected in 1856. It was to him that young Custer applied for an appointment. The elder Custer was a Democrat, a "Jacksonian" Democrat, and remained such all his life. His sons were trained in that political faith. So far as he had anything to do with politics, there is reason to believe that Armstrong Custer was true to the political principles of his father, Emmanuel Custer. Indeed, the old gentleman averred with much emphasis when asked if the general was not a Democrat—

"Of course he was a Democrat. My boys were all Democrats. I would not raise any other kind."

It is not strange, therefore, that the father gave the son no encouragement when he proposed to ask Congressman Bingham for a cadetship. He did not believe that a Republican congressman would thus favor the son of a Democrat of the Emmanuel Custer stripe.[11]

But the future major general of division was not to be deterred by that or any other trifling obstacles from making the effort. With the faith in himself which he ever afterwards displayed, in May, 1856, he wrote to Mr. Bingham a most frank and manly letter asking him for an appointment, expressing the belief that he could meet the requirements and offering to furnish certificates of good moral character. But another had the call that year, and the next year he went to Mr. Bingham in person and made an impression so favorable upon the mind of the congressman that he won his heart and confidence at once, and received the appointment.

In this way it came about that in June, 1857, Custer entered the West Point Military Academy, the protégé of Hon. John Bingham, afterwards minister to Japan, who was thus instrumental in starting on his military course one of the real heroes of the nation.

The career of Cadet Custer in West Point was not a remarkable one. In point of scholarship he just managed to keep within the breastworks. Like Ulysses S. Grant, he did not stand anywhere near the head of his class. Like Grant, he was a splendid horseman and well liked. He said himself that in a class numbering thirty-five members, who were graduated, he was thirty-fourth. This was from no lack of ability, for he mastered his studies with the greatest ease, but because he was so full of exuberant animal spirits, of fun and frolic, that he was continually getting demerit marks for some venial infraction of the rules of conduct and discipline. He was a favorite and won the hearts of all by his good nature, his manliness and high sense of honor, all of which however, did not keep him out of mischief; or prevent his paying the penalty for dereliction, in loss of class standing and the privileges that fell to "prize" cadets.

Custer's notification of his appointment came from Jefferson Davis, then Secretary of War in Buchanan's cabinet;[12] the commandant of the academy was John F. Reynolds, afterwards major general of volunteers killed at Gettysburg.[13] One of his instructors was Fitzhugh Lee.[14] In the corps of cadets were many young men of the south, two of whom, Thomas L. Rosser, of Virginia, and P. M. B. Young,[15] of Georgia, became major generals of Confederate cavalry; with whom Custer crossed swords on many battle fields.

When the time came for the class to be graduated, June, 1861, and the cadets assigned to the various branches of the military service, war had broken out between the states, a southern Confederacy had been formed, and two armies—one for the Union, the other against it—were assembling in Virginia to submit the question of union or disunion to the arbitrament of arms. The southerners went home to their several states and cast their lots with the Confederacy. The northern boys eagerly sought service in the armies of the United States to fight for the Union under the Stars and Stripes. Among these last, none were more patriotic and enthusiastic than was young Custer. But his career came near to being nipped in the bud, through one of those characteristic breaches of discipline just on the eve of graduation. He was an officer of the guard, when the order from Washington designating the cadets as officers of the army was hourly expected. The way in which the impulses of the boy overcame the official obligation of the officer of the guard, during his tour of duty in that position is best described in his own language:

"Just at dark I heard a commotion near the guard tents. Hastening to the scene, I found two cadets engaged in a dispute which threatened to result in blows. A group of cadets had formed about the two bellicose disputants. I had hardly time to take in the situation, when the two disputants began belaboring each other with their fists. Some of their more prudent friends rushed in and sought to separate the two antagonists. My duty was plain. I should have arrested the combatants and sent them to the guardhouse for violating the peace and regulations of the academy. But the instincts of the boy prevailed over the obligations of the officer. I pushed my way through the line of cadets, dashed back those who were interfering with the struggle and called out: 'Stand back, boys, let's have a fair fight.'"[16]

The result of this breach of duty was that Cadet Custer was sent to his tent in arrest, charges were preferred, and sent on to Washington. A court martial was convened to try him on the charges and, when his classmates went to Washington for assignment as officers of the army, he was left behind in arrest, awaiting the outcome of the court martial's findings, which were promptly forwarded to the war department.

But when his classmates arrived in Washington, they interceded for him. The government was in sore need of educated officers, and a telegraphic order was sent for his release and directing him to report to the War Department, forthwith, for assignment to duty.

It will be necessary owing to the limitations of space, to pass rapidly over the life of Custer as a subaltern in the Regular Army. He arrived in Washington July 20, 1861, and reporting to General Scott, was ordered to join his troop of the Second United States Cavalry on duty with General McDowell's army,[17] at the front. General Scott also entrusted him with important dispatches to General McDowell—a most auspicious beginning for a youngster just out of West Point. With much difficulty he succeeded in reaching the front and delivered the dispatches. He joined and with the rank of second lieutenant was engaged with his troop at Bull Run, the first battle of the war. That was July 21, just one day after his arrival in Washington. Thus, there was no interval between the time of reporting for duty and the beginning of his active service in the field; and that service was practically continuous not only until the day of his death, June 25, 1876—barely fifteen years almost to a day—yet how full of heroism and achievement was that short period of an American army officer's life.

Custer was at that time but little more than twenty-one years of age. There was an indefinable something about his personality that attracted the attention of his superiors in years and rank. His courage was conspicuous, and from the first, opportunity came his way, and the phrase, "Custer's luck" was often on his own lips; but the secret of his phenomenal rise as a cavalry officer must be sought elsewhere than in mere luck. He was resolute, alert, and ambitious. He possessed a certain prescience or intuition which pointed out the way and taught him what to do and when to do it.

Whatever was given him to do, whether in high or low station, he did with all his might. His motto seemed to be, "Make myself as useful as possible in the performance of every duty." In this he succeeded so well that his superiors found they could not well get along without him.

Soon after the battle of Bull Run, Custer received a detail as an aide-de-camp to General Philip Kearny,[18] one of the ablest and most picturesque officers of the Civil War. Straightway, he was designated as assistant adjutant general of the brigade. He made good, as he never failed to do, won the confidence of his chief, and remained on Kearny's staff until the war department ruled that regular army officers could no longer be permitted on the staffs of generals of volunteers.

In the spring of 1862, Custer was transferred from the Second to the Fifth United States Cavalry without increased rank. In the Peninsular campaign he was selected as an engineer officer at the headquarters of General W. F. ("Baldy") Smith.[19] He was mentioned for gallantry in a report of General W. S. Hancock;[20] was especially commended for zealous and brave conduct by General Barnard,[21] chief engineer of the Army of the Potomac; and finally, a characteristic exploit brought him to the favorable notice of General George B. McClellan[22] who, as a reward, appointed him on his staff with the rank of captain. Thus, in less than a year from graduation, he found himself a trusted member of the staff of the commander-in-chief of the army. His commission as captain was signed by President Lincoln and forwarded to him by Secretary of War, Edwin M. Stanton. It was dated June 5, 1862. He served in this capacity during the seven days battles; through the Antietam campaign and until the retirement of "Little Mac" from the command; signalizing his service by frequent deeds of daring that brought him more and more into favorable attention. And Custer was then a boy of twenty-two. During the winter of 1862-63 he was with his chief in retirement; assisting the latter in the work of making his voluminous report of the operations of the army while under his command. In the spring of 1863 he was ordered back to his regiment, the Fifth Cavalry, then on duty with Burnside[23] near Falmouth. Captain Custer was once more Lieutenant Custer, though the former title stuck to him and he was spoken of always as "Captain Custer."

During that year it became known that two regiments of cavalry, the Sixth and Seventh, were to be raised in Michigan and Captain Custer applied to Governor Blair[24] for the colonelcy of one of them.[25] His application was refused and he had to be content with his lower rank. He did not remain long with this regiment, for he was detailed successively as aide-de-camp on the staff of General Buford,[26] chief of the First Cavalry Division, and of General Pleasonton,[27] chief of cavalry. With the latter, as with Kearny and McClellan, he was a great favorite. He had tact, energy, intuition, the ability to grasp the elusive opportunity, courage of the highest type and, in every engagement, he was in the very forefront. In the battle of Aldie,[28] though but a lieutenant, he rode side by side with Colonel Kilpatrick,[29] commander of a brigade, and Colonel Douty,[30] of the First Maine Cavalry, in leading a successful charge against Stuart's Confederate troopers. Douty was killed and Kilpatrick wounded. Custer came out without a scratch. It may be surmised that Pleasonton made a note of the gallant conduct of his young aide and, as a matter of fact, in that very month, Custer, upon Pleasonton's recommendation, was promoted from lieutenant in the Fifth Cavalry to brigadier general of volunteers. His commission was dated June 29, 1863. He was assigned to command the Second Brigade, Third Division of the Cavalry Corps. Kilpatrick was at the same time made general of division. Elon J. Farnsworth, of the Eighth Illinois Cavalry, received his star on the same day and was placed in command of the First Brigade.[31]

The Michigan Cavalry Brigade (Second Brigade, Third Division) consisted of four regiments—the First, Fifth, Sixth, and Seventh. The First went out in 1861 under Colonel T. F. Brodhead, a veteran of the Mexican War, who was killed in the Second Battle of Bull Run.[32] The Fifth, Sixth, and Seventh were organized a year later and had been serving in the Department of Washington. The brigade only recently had been organized and was on duty in Fairfax County, Virginia, when Hooker[33] began his march into Maryland to head off the Army of Northern Virginia under Lee, which had begun an invasion of the north similar to that which ended so disastrously to him and his army at the battle of Antietam in 1862. The Michigan regiments left Fairfax Courthouse and, crossing the Potomac River at Edwards Ferry, marched via Poolesville, Frederick, and Emmitsburg to Gettysburg, arriving in that town—destined so soon to give its name to one of the greatest battles of history—on Sunday, June 28, 1863. Thence they were concentrated at Hanover, a few miles southeast of Gettysburg, as a part of the force sent under Kilpatrick to intercept the march of Stuart's cavalry which was groping its way, three brigades strong,[34] in search of Lee's army, from which it had been separated since the beginning of the campaign. Coming successively into the little village of Hanover, under the command of their respective colonels, they were dismounted to fight on foot, and deploying into line, facing the southeast, advanced through some wheat fields towards the heights whereon were placed Stuart's brigades under Hampton, Chambliss, and Fitzhugh Lee. The Michigan men, with the exception of the First Cavalry, never had been under fire. It was their first battle. Suddenly there appeared upon the scene a picturesque figure whom none of them had ever seen. This was the young brigadier general just twenty-three years and six months old, who had worn his star but two days. He was a stranger to them; they were strangers to him.

Instantly, order began to come out of the disorder that had prevailed for several hours. He gave his orders in clear, resonant tones, at once resolute and reassuring. At first he was thought to be a staff officer conveying the commands of his chief, but in a very short time it became apparent that he himself was the commander. It will not be amiss to give here a pen sketch of him as he appeared to an officer just three months his junior in years who happened to be in command of a troop upon the very part of the line where he was.[†]

"Looking at him closely this is what I saw: An officer superbly mounted who sat his charger as if 'to the manor born'. Tall, lithe, active, muscular, straight as an Indian and as quick in his movements, he had the fair complexion of a school girl. He was uniformed in a suit of black velvet, elaborately trimmed with gold lace which ran down the outer seams of his trousers and almost covered the sleeves of his cavalry jacket. The wide collar of a blue navy shirt with embroidered stars at the points, was turned over the collar of his velvet jacket, and a necktie of bright crimson was tied in a graceful know at the throat, the long ends falling carelessly in front. The double rows of brass buttons on his breast were arranged in groups of twos, indicating the rank of brigadier general. A soft black hat with wide brim adorned with a gilt cord, and a rosette encircling a silver star, was worn turned down on one side, giving him a rakish air. His golden hair fell in graceful luxuriance nearly or quite to his shoulders and his upper lip was garnished with a blonde mustache. A sword and belt, gilt spurs and top boots completed his unique outfit.

"A keen eye would have been slow to detect in that rider with the flowing locks and bright necktie, in his dress of velvet and gold, the master

---

[†]*Personal Recollections of a Cavalryman*, by J. H. Kidd.

spirit that he proved to be. That garb, fantastic as at first sight it appeared, was to be the distinguishing mark that, like the white plume of Henry of Navarre,[35] was to show us where in the thickest of the fight we were to seek our leader—for where danger was, where swords were to cross, where Greek met Greek, there was he always. Brave, but not reckless; self-confident yet modest; ambitious but regulating his conduct at all times by a high code of honor and duty; eager for laurels, but scorning to wear them unworthily; ready and willing to act, but regardful of human life; quick in emergencies, cool and self-poised, his courage was of the highest moral and physical type, his perceptions were intuitions. Showy, like Murat, fiery like Kearny, yet calm and self reliant like Sheridan, he was the most brilliant and resourceful cavalry officer of his time. Such a man had appeared upon the scene and from that day the Michigan cavalrymen swore by Custer and would follow him to the death."

"George Armstrong Custer was undeniably the most picturesque figure of the Civil War. Yet his ability and services were hardly justly appraised by the American people. It is doubtful if more than one of his superior officers—if we except Kearny, McClellan and Pleasonton, who knew him only as a subaltern—estimated him at his true value. Sheridan knew him for what he was. So did the Michigan Cavalry Brigade and the Third Cavalry Division. Except by these he was regarded as a brave and dashing but reckless officer who needed a steady hand to guide him. Among regular army officers he cannot be said to have been a favorite. The rapidity of his rise to the zenith of his fame and unexampled success, when so many of the youngsters of his years were moving in the comparative obscurity of their own orbits, irritated them. Stars of the first magnitude did not appear often in the galaxy of heroes. Custer was one of the few."

"The popular idea of Custer is a misconception. He was not a reckless commander. He was not regardless of human life. No man could have been more careful of the lives and comfort of his men. His heart was as tender as that of a woman. He was kind to his subordinates, tolerant of their weaknesses, ever ready to help and encourage them. He was as brave as a lion, fought as few men fought, but from no love of fighting. That was his business, and he knew that in that way alone peace could be conquered. He was brave, alert, untiring, a hero in battle, relentless in the pursuit of a beaten enemy, stubborn and full of resources in a retreat. His death at the battle of the Little Big Horn crowned his career with a tragic interest that will not wane while history or tradition endure. Hundreds of brave men

In Grant's great campaign of 1864—from the Wilderness, May 6, to Cold Harbor, June 1—he was the bright, particular star in that constellation of heroes who rode with Sheridan. His intrepid spirit never flagged and, "where'er the bravest dared to be" the sabers of his Michigan cavalry were seen. On the left flank in the Wilderness, he met and vanquished Rosser, the brave southern cavalryman, so completely that his dead and wounded were left in our hands on the field; thus warding off the expected flanking attack so much dreaded by Meade, Grant, and Hancock. May 7, he aided Gregg[46] in defeating those brave knights of the Southern cause, Stuart and Fitzhugh Lee.

He led the advance on Sheridan's great raid into the enemy's country, when ten thousand horse cut loose from the Army of the Potomac and, in a column thirteen miles long, sought out Stuart and challenged him to a fight to the finish upon his native heath. Detached from the main column Custer captured Beaver Dam Station, recaptured several hundred Union prisoners who were being rushed to Richmond, and destroyed an immense quantity of Lee's military stores, including all of his medical supplies.

On the morning of May 11, at Yellow Tavern, six miles north of Richmond, at the critical moment in the battle, Custer was entrusted with the important duty of making a mounted charge against the enemy strongly posted on a commanding ridge flanked by artillery. He penetrated the enemy's line with the First and Seventh Michigan mounted and supported by the Fifth and Sixth on foot; captured one of his batteries and, in the melee that resulted, the Confederate leader, Stuart, the prince of Southern cavaliers, was killed and his entire body of cavalry put to rout.[47] The next day, May 12, Custer was selected by Sheridan[48] to open the way across the Chickahominy, at the Meadow Bridges, the only gateway to safety from the somewhat critical position in which he found himself. The bridge had been destroyed and, Fitzhugh Lee, who succeeded Stuart, had taken up and fortified a naturally strong defensive position on the opposite shore. Passing the Fifth and Sixth Michigan across on the ties of a railroad bridge, Custer gained a foothold, drove Lee's skirmishers into their breastworks, and rebuilt the bridge, so that Sheridan passed his entire force across it in safety, after Gregg had repulsed a menacing attack in rear, led by Jefferson Davis in person.

On the return from the neighborhood around Richmond to the army at Chesterfield Station, which occupied the time until May 26, Custer was constantly called upon to perform special and important service, showing that the confidence which he had inspired in his chief was absolute. Stopping,

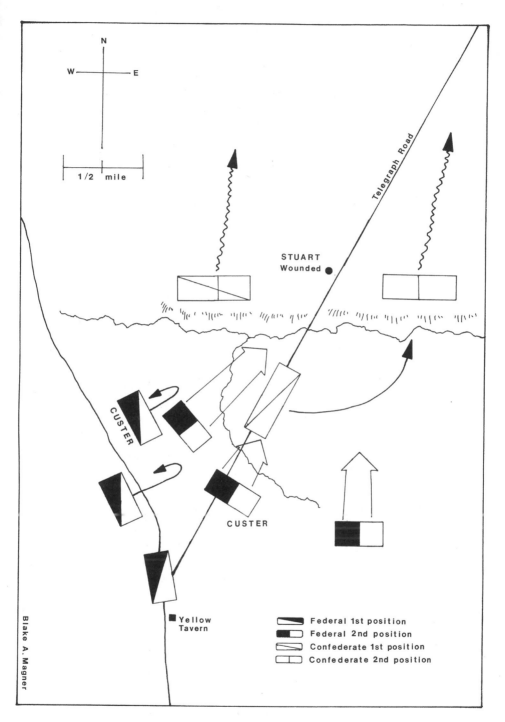

The Battle of Yellow Tavern, May 11, 1864

on one of these side expeditions, at a house where were many ladies of
Southern proclivities, he wrote and entrusted to the care of one of them a
chivalrous message to his friend, P. M. B. Young, a classmate in West Point.
Young had made a prophecy at the mess table one day before they left the
Academy that each would be a colonel of a cavalry regiment from his state—
Custer from Michigan, Young from Georgia—and that they would meet
in battle. The prophecy had been more than fulfilled. Each had command
of a brigade and they had met more than once in battle. Custer told Young
he wished that he would stay in one place long enough to be found; that he
had been hot on his trail for many day but could not overtake him and
bring him to a fight. The lady promised to deliver the letter and did so.
After the war, the two cavalry officers met and were good friends, as before.

May 27, Custer again led the advance of the army, in the movement
across the Pamunkey into the country between that river and the
Chickahominy. He forced the crossing at Hanovertown with the First Michigan, then advanced toward Hanover Court House, the Sixth Michigan
leading. Soon, Gordon's brigade of North Carolinians,[49] under Barringer,[50]
Gordon having been killed, was encountered and a hard fight ensued.
Putting the First and Sixth Michigan into action dismounted, he took the
Fifth and Seventh and leading them in person around the flank of the
force confronting the other regiments put it to rout, the pursuit taking
him to Crump's Creek, several miles away. When he went into this charge,
he set his band playing Yankee Doodle, which had the effect to put an end
for the occasion to the music of the Confederate band which had been
playing Bonnie Blue Flag, in rear of their line.

The next day at Haw's Shop occurred the hardest and most bloody cavalry fight of the entire war, numbers engaged considered. Gregg, with the
Second Division of but two brigades had been sent out to uncover the
movements of Lee's army. He had advanced but a short distance beyond
Haw's Shop when he ran into the entire Confederate cavalry force under
Wade Hampton, who had succeeded Stuart. Gregg was getting the worst
of it and called for help. The Michigan brigade was ordered to the front as
a reinforcement. Coming into the engagement from the rear and about
opposite to Gregg's center, Custer formed the brigade, dismounted in double
ranks, and riding ahead of the line, accompanied by a single aide, waved his
hat over his head and called for three cheers. The cheers were given and he
led his men in a charge into the woods where Butler's South Carolinians[51]
were just coming into action on the other side. Then it was face to face, eye

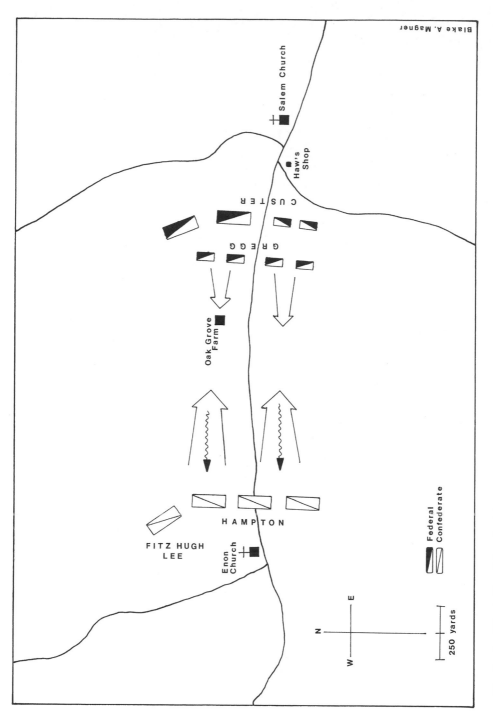

Salem Church

Haw's Shop

C U S T E R

G R E G G

Oak Grove Farm

FITZ HUGH LEE

Enon Church

H A M P T O N

Federal
Confederate

N
W — E
S

250 yards

The Battle of Haw's Shop, May 28, 1864

to eye. The effect of Custer's splendid courage was to inspire his Wolverines to more than their wonted bravery. In a few minutes the men from the Palmetto State were in headlong flight, leaving their dead and wounded. About one hundred officers and men were killed and wounded in the Michigan Brigade and it all befell within a very few minutes after the charge into the woods. The ground was covered with Confederate dead. The trees were riddled with bullets. The leaden hail, hitting the bushes and bark of the trees, sounded like crackling glass. The sound of the firing was heard distinctly far to the rear, where Grant, Meade, and Sheridan anxiously were awaiting the event. Custer with his usual luck, escaped without a wound. His aide was shot in two places. He there made a record for personal daring and magnetic leadership unsurpassed on either side during the Civil War. Ah, but he was a gallant and inspiring figure, dressed as at Hanover, his blonde curls flying, his red necktie flaming, riding his horse in front of his men on foot—between them and the enemy who, with undaunted front, were firing as fast as they could load and daring him to come on. No more brave deed was ever done. Haw's Shop stamped Custer—and not Custer only but the men who followed him into that sanguinary hell of fire, as he dashed into the thickest of it—as "the bravest of the brave." He saved Gregg's division. He won the battle. He vanquished the very flower of the southern cavaliers. No more, after Haw's Shop, were heard those cruel and unjust words: "Whoever saw a dead cavalryman?"

At Haw's Shop, as at Gettysburg, Custer and his brigade came opportunely to the relief of Gregg's splendid division. Upon those two battles alone, if there had been no other, their fame rests as secure as that of Cardigan[52] and the Light Brigade for their charge at Balaklava.[53] Here is a theme as noble as that which inspired the British bard, and soon or late, some American Tennyson, will sing of Custer and the Michigan Brigade at Rummel's farm or at Haw's Shop, in verse as heroic as that of the English poet in "The Charge of the Light Brigade."

Haw's Shop led up to Cold Harbor. Indeed, it was the beginning of that bloody struggle which Grant in his memoirs seems to apologize for as one that ought never to have been fought. The afternoon of May 31, the Michigan and Reserve Brigades[54]—Custer and Merritt—drove the Confederate cavalry out of Cold Harbor and took possession of the place. The Federal infantry was ten miles away. The Confederate infantry was concentrating in front of the Federal cavalry and Sheridan, believing that he could not hold the position, directed Sheridan to return and hold it all hazards until the infantry could come up. Then followed one of the most remarkable features of that unexampled campaign. From midnight May 31 until noon June 1, a thin line of dismounted cavalry, behind a slight barrier of rails, with artillery in action close behind them, held off the Confederate infantry in strong force. Then the Sixth Corps came up and relieved them and the battle of Cold Harbor had begun. At reveille, that morning, the bugles of the enemy sounded close in front, the commands of the officers were heard distinctly. It seemed that at any moment they would charge right over that attenuated line. But the bold front of the cavalry completely deceived them. Custer was as usual the most conspicuous figure. Riding along the line, from right to left and from left to right again, he spoke encouraging words to his officers and men lying behind those piles of rails; inspiring them by his example and making them think they were invincible. Custer always was on horseback. He never was seen on foot in battle, even when every other officer and man in his command was dismounted. And he rode close to the very front line, fearless and resolute. When advancing against an enemy, he was with the skirmishers; on the retreat, he rode with the rear guard. Those who had occasion to seek him out in battle, found him in the place nearest the enemy. Such was he at Gettysburg, at Brandy Station, at Buckland Mills, in the Wilderness, at Haw's Shop, and at Cold Harbor. By this time, the reason for his choosing so singular a uniform was seen. It individualized him. Wherever seen, it was recognized. There was but one Custer, and by his unique appearance and heroic bearing he was readily distinguished from all others.

Then came Trevilian Station, that battle about which so much has been written and so little of the truth is really known. Grant had determined, after the terrible carnage in and around Cold Harbor, to make another movement by the left flank and shift the position of his entire army from the Pamunkey to the James. Sheridan was directed to take two divisions of his cavalry and proceed leisurely to Charlottesville on the Virginia Central Railroad. The object of this raid was two fold: To draw away the Confederate cavalry while the transfer was being made and to effect a junction with Hunter,[55] who with a considerable force of infantry was operating between Charlottesville and Lynchburg. If successful in this, they were jointly to advance and capture Lynchburg. Sheridan's march began with the First and Second Divisions (Torbert[56] and Gregg) by crossing the Pamunkey at Newcastle Ferry June 7, and going thence by easy stages along the north bank of the North Anna River, reaching Carpenter's Ford the night of June 10. Then he crossed and camped on the road leading past Clayton's Store to Trevilian Station. Trevilian is a station on the railroad between Louisa Courthouse and Gordonsville.

As soon as Sheridan's movement was known, Hampton was with two divisions of cavalry (his own and Fitzhugh Lee's), five brigades,[57] moved parallel with Sheridan's march and on the south side of the river. He reached Trevilian Station the same night that Sheridan camped at Clayton's Store. Breckinridge's[58] corps of infantry started the same time as Hampton, and succeeded in reaching Gordonsville. Thus Sheridan had in his front, between him and Hunter, to meet his two divisions of cavalry, two divisions of cavalry, and a corps on infantry. Moreover, Hunter instead of seeking to effect a junction, finding that he was intercepted, was marching the other way. It will be seen that, with no prospect of help from Hunter, Sheridan was easily "an unequal match for Achilles."

But Hampton made one fatal blunder. On the night of June 10 his command was separated. He was in Trevilian Station with three brigades of cavalry. Fitzhugh Lee was at Louisa Courthouse seven miles away with two brigades. Breckinridge was at or near Gordonsville. Hampton planned to advance from Trevilian Station to Clayton's Store on the morning of June 11 and attack Sheridan. Fitzhugh Lee was to march by another road and unite with Hampton. Sheridan advanced from Clayton's Store toward Trevilian Station to meet Hampton. The two lines met midway and a fierce battle resulted.

Custer with the Michigan Brigade had been in camp and picketing toward Louisa Courthouse. He was ordered to take a country road and come into the station from a direction different from that taken by Torbert with the rest of the First Division and one brigade of Gregg's division. The other brigade of the Second Division was sent out toward Louisa Courthouse and intercepted Fitzhugh Lee, preventing his junction with Hampton. Custer also got between Lee and Hampton, around the latter's right flank into his rear, and captured a large number of his led horses and some of his trains, the capture being made by a charge of the Fifth Michigan Cavalry.

In the meantime, the fight was raging between Hampton and Torbert. Fitzhugh Lee was making a detour by still another road leading to the station. All the roads converged to that one point.

When Hampton heard the tumult to his rear, caused by the Fifth Michigan, he recalled Rosser's Brigade,[59] which had been posted to protect his left flank, and the latter came into action in time to cut off the Fifth Michigan. The Sixth Michigan charged and drove away a portion of Young's Brigade of Hampton's Division, which interposed between Custer and the Fifth

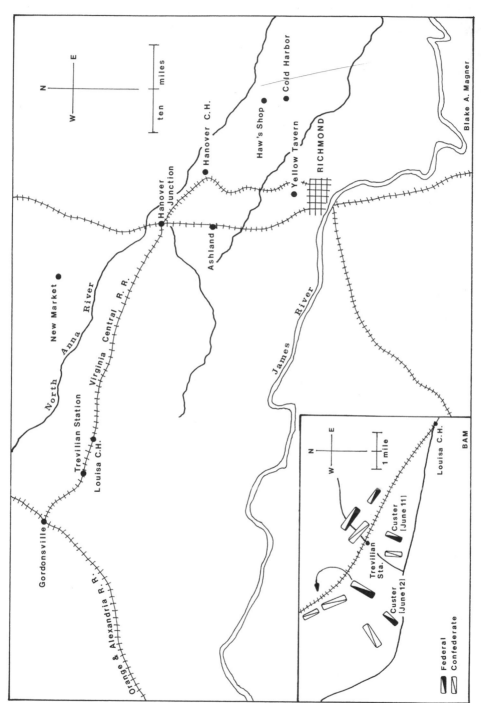

Sheridan's Trevilian Station Raid, June 11–12, 1864

Michigan after the latter's charge. The First and Seventh Michigan, which had been out on the road to Louisa Courthouse, returned and Custer proceeded toward Trevilian, arriving just in time to encounter Rosser on his front and right flank and Fitzhugh Lee coming in on the road from Louisa Courthouse on his left flank; while another force, the identity of which is not certain, attacked his rear. He was surrounded. His line for a time was in the form of a circle.[60] Then it was that he was seen at his best. One gun of Pennington's Battery was charged by Fitzhugh Lee and was taken. Custer made a counter charge and retook it. The fighting was hand to hand. He was everywhere present. First in front and then in rear, again on either flank. His color bearer was shot and to prevent the colors falling into the hands of the enemy he tore from the staff and carried them to a place of safety. He was now in rear of Young's and Butler's brigades and Torbert was driving them back upon him. But Rosser being in his front, Fitzhugh Lee on his left flank and rear, the problem was to hold them off until Torbert could break through to his aid. The latter was finally successful in doing this. The two divisions united at last. Hampton was driven to the west, Fitzhugh Lee to the east, and they failed in their effort to come together. Custer's bulldog courage alone prevented it.

The next day Sheridan advanced toward Gordonsville, Custer and his brigade leading. A few miles out the Confederate cavalry was found dismounted and entrenched. An engagement remarkable for its stubbornness followed. Hampton demonstrated that he was a hard fighter, as he had done at Haw's Shop. Fitzhugh Lee succeeded in reinforcing him at a critical moment, and it was believed at the time that Sheridan had some of Breckinridge's infantry from Gordonsville in his front, also. But that is doubtful. Custer's attack was vigorous and persistent, but not successful. The battle lasted all day and well into the night. The Confederates never fought better and their losses were very heavy, including in the list of killed and wounded many officers of high rank. General Rosser was one of the wounded.[61] Custer's conduct of his part of the affair was brilliant in the extreme. His losses were greater than in any other engagement of the campaign, with the exception of Haw's Shop. That night, Sheridan retreated and rejoined the army. He had not succeeded in taking Lynchburg or in finding Hunter, but he had relieved the Army of the Potomac of the presence of the troublesome Confederate cavalry while it was accomplishing its change of base.

The planning and fighting of the battle, with its artful maneuvers and tactical stratagems, have been compared to a game of chess. To my mind, no cavalry engagement of the Civil War had more points of resemblance to the moves of knights and pawns upon the chessboard than did the first day at Trevilian Station. Custer is said to have been a lover of the game of chess. If so, he certainly never found more difficulty in achieving a checkmate than when he attacked Hampton's rear only to find himself "checked" by Fitzhugh Lee's sudden appearance in his own rear. Both played the game with much skill but there was no checkmate at last. It was a drawn game, brilliantly though Custer played it.

Most of the month of June, 1864, was consumed in the return march to the army. July was a month of comparative exemption from the strenuous and dangerous operations which had fallen to the cavalry, and which extended over a period of fifty-six days of constant marching and fighting, oftentimes by night and day. From May 6 to June 12, Custer's brigade lost 148 officers and men killed. From May 6 to June 26 it lost 269 killed and wounded. Thirty-three were killed at Yellow Tavern; forty-two at Haw's Shop; forty-one at Trevilian Station; one hundred and sixteen in the three battles. Custer himself was not even wounded.

August 3, Custer and his Michigan Brigade bade farewell to the Army of the Potomac, and embarking on transports, steamed away to Washington, whence they marched to the Shenandoah Valley, arriving at Halltown, in front of Harper's Ferry, August 10, in time to take part in the forward movement of the army of the "Middle Military Division"—a new department including West Virginia, the Shenandoah Valley and Harper's Ferry—over which General Sheridan was to exercise supreme command.

The Shenandoah Valley Campaign of 1864, which began August 10 and ended October 19, at Cedar Creek, a period of but seventy days, was epochal in its importance. Its results were far reaching. It marked the beginning of the end of the tragedy of the Civil War. After Cedar Creek, the Valley was no longer tenable by a hostile force. This storehouse of the Confederacy had been stripped clean of everything that could contribute to the maintenance of an army. To use Grant's expressive phrase: "A crow flying over this region will have to carry its own rations."[62] Grant had nothing to fear from that direction. Thenceforth the Confederacy was but an empty shell, about which that silent soldier gradually tightened his iron grip until he crushed it at Appomattox.

Sheridan was the real hero of the epoch. He did his work thoroughly and well. Through it all, Custer was his right arm. He it was who struck the hardest and most effective blows. At Front Royal, August 16, his genius flashed out like a shining star when, after checking Fitzhugh Lee's cavalry, he caught the head of Anderson's Division[63] of infantry amid stream as it was fording the Shenandoah River and smashed it, capturing hundreds of prisoners. At Shepherdstown,[64] August 25, when left in the lurch by Torbert, and surrounded by Breckinridge's infantry, he extricated his brigade from its perilous position by the most imperturbable coolness and brilliant strategy. At Winchester September 19, he charged across the Opequon Creek in the face of infantry sharpshooters behind piles of rails. He charged, mounted, upon infantry lines behind stone fences. From early in the morning he kept up a running and relentless pursuit. He scattered Early's mounted cavalry like leaves before a blast. He paused not for volleys of musketry or enfilading artillery fire. At the last, he "rushed like a whirlwind" down a slope upon swarms of infantry on the open plain and, his red necktie troopers close behind him, captured more prisoners than he had officers and men under him.

Here will I pause. That was the last great battle in which Custer led the Michigan Brigade. Alas! and alas! He was to be our leader no longer. Thenceforth the Wolverines must fain be content to serve under others, fated to look on with sad faces while the troopers of other states followed the red and blue emblem in the places which had known them no more forever. That, however, was no fault of General Custer. He wanted to take his old brigade with him into the Third Cavalry Division. There is plenty of evidence of that. He hoped and expected that the transfer would be made. But through some mysterious and malign influence this was prevented. It was an open secret, however, at the time, that Sheridan had given Custer what the latter believed to be an assurance that his wishes were to be respected.

Winchester singled Custer out for a higher command. September 26, Averell[65] having been relieved from command of the Second Division, Custer was ordered to take his place. But before he could reach his new command, James H. Wilson[66] was sent to Sherman[67] in the west, and Custer placed in command of the Third Division. It was the Third Division which had won such honors under Kilpatrick the previous year with Custer and Davies as its brigade commanders. But Davies[68] had gone to the Second Division when Custer went to the First, and the old Third, the same only in name, had lost much of its elan. In the campaign of 1864 it had to be content to follow where others led. From the Rapidan to the James, the First Division had been "the lancehead of the cavalry." What a change! Under Custer the Third Division came to its own again. It was now the "lancehead." From Tom's

Brook[69] to Waynesborough[70]; and from Winchester to Appomattox[71]—at Sailor's Creek,[72] at Five Forks,[73] everywhere during the quick, effective and one-sided campaign of 1865—the Third Division was always in advance— the avenging force that, with inexorable persistence, flew at the fleeing and disintegrating columns of the Confederate armies, driving Lee to bay, at last, and compelling his surrender. It was Custer who was first at the death. It was Custer who clipped the brush. He received the flag of truce. He won this high commendation from Sheridan that no man deserved more than he from his country for his part in the closing scenes of the war tragedy.

Custer's spectacular ride in the "grand review" formed a fitting finale to his record in the Civil War. The president of the United States, the Congress, the Supreme Court, the cabinet, the heads of departments, high dignitaries both civil and military, ambassadors and ministers of foreign nations, were assembled in the immense grand stand, in front of the White House to witness the greatest military pageant of modern times, if not of all times. The great army of Grant and the great army of Sherman were to pass in review. Pennsylvania Avenue, from the Capitol to the White House, and far beyond in either direction, was lined on both sides with an eager and enthusiastic multitude of spectators, numbering hundreds of thousands.

On the first day, Custer, riding at the head of his division, which led the parade, picturesque, if not spectacular to the last, bestrode a thorough bred stallion, named Don Juan, captured in North Carolina and valued at ten thousand dollars. The horse, more accustomed to the bucolic quietude of his rural harem than to the bustle and roar of Pennsylvania Avenue at such a time as that, finally took fright at the demonstrations made in honor of his ride and ran away. Beyond control, he rushed like "Black Auster" up the avenue. Between the lines of wondering people, past the Treasury Building, past the grand stand, he sped in his mad career, and was not checked until he had passed out of sight. Custer did not forget to salute as he "looked toward" the amazed spectators on the reviewing stand.

Here this sketch might fittingly end. The statue is a memorial of him as an officer of volunteers in the Civil War. The book for which this is written is a souvenir of the statue and its dedication. But, inasmuch as the president of the United States in his address at the unveiling treated of Custer as an officer of Regulars in Indian warfare, on the plains, I venture in conclusion to touch briefly upon Custer's Last Fight.

The reorganization of the Regular Army which followed the Civil War found Custer lieutenant colonel of the Seventh Cavalry, a new regiment.[74]

The officers, field and line, were for the most part in not entirely, men who had served in the volunteers, many of them with much higher rank. The actual command of the regiment fell to Custer, as the colonel never joined it.[75] During the ten years—from 1866 to 1876—under the influence of his personality the Seventh Cavalry made a record which equaled, if it did not surpass, the best traditions of the old Army.[76] During that period the Indian question became acute and there were constant outbreaks of the red men, while the little force of Regulars on duty on the plains had more than it could do to keep the "hostiles" in subjection.

In this Indian warfare Custer and his regiment, like Custer and the Third Cavalry Division in the last campaign of the Civil War, were easily foremost. He was the most successful Indian fighter of his day, and was so regarded by all the military authorities.[77] For this reason when a campaign was determined upon to end the Indian troubles, he was looked upon as the proper leader.

The plan of the campaign projected for the discomfiture of the hostile Indians was to advance against them from three directions, with three isolated columns having no means of intercommunication, the idea being to surround them and prevent their "escape."[78] One of these columns was to start from Fort Lincoln, Dakota; one from Fort Ellis in Western Montana; the other from Fort Fetterman on the Platte River in northern Wyoming. The first column was to be commanded by General Custer; the second by General Gibbon;[79] the third by General Crook;[80] all under the command of General Terry,[81] department commander. Neither General Sherman at Washington, General Sheridan at Chicago, nor General Terry at St. Paul had any exact knowledge of the numbers of location of the hostile force which it was their purpose to corral. General Terry and General Gibbon were infantry officers with slight experience in Indian warfare and scant knowledge of the country in which they were to operate. Crook, like Custer, had seen service in the Indian country but, unlike Custer, had not distinguished himself by any marked success as an Indian fighter. Terry was personally to command the Fort Lincoln column of which the Seventh Cavalry under Lieutenant Colonel Custer was part.

Crook's force in round numbers consisted of about 1,300 officers and men; Gibbon's of 400; Terry's of 1,000; not exceeding 2,700 all told. The estimates made at the headquarters of the army did not place the fighting strength of the hostiles as more than 500 to 800 warriors. The effective strength of the Seventh Cavalry did not much exceed 600.[82] Custer on the eve of his departure from the Yellowstone thought he might meet 1,000, possibly 1,500 fighting Indians. But he seems to have been alone in that opinion. The higher military authorities, from General Sherman down to General Terry, believed that either of the isolated columns could defeat the Indians. The only thing they feared was that they might get away. The only precautions to be taken were such as would prevent their "escape." There was nowhere a hint of apprehension that the Indians might get the better of the troops that were being sent against them. In his last order to Custer, dated June 22, 1876, Terry enjoined him thus:

"Should it (the trail) be found to turn towards the Little Big Horn, you should proceed southward, perhaps as far as the headwaters of the Tongue, and then turn towards the Little Horn, feeling constantly to your left, so as to preclude the possibility of the escape of the Indians by passing around your left flank."

And again:

"It is hoped that the Indians may be so nearly enclosed by the two columns (Custer's and Gibbon's) that their escape will be impossible."

Thus, when Custer started on his last ride the only fear that his immediate superior appeared to have was that he might permit the Indians to pass "around his left flank" and make their "escape." Not a hint of apprehension about the safety of his own command. Terry did not dream that more than 500 to 800 warriors would be encountered and his instructions contained in his final order were explicit and could not be misinterpreted. Custer was to go in "pursuit" of the Indians and prevent their "escape." Yet, at the funeral of General Terry, the pastor who preached the sermon, giving as his authority Colonel Hughes,[83] Terry's brother-in-law and personal aide, charged that Custer disobeyed Terry's orders and recklessly rushed upon his own fate. A more cruel and unwarranted charge never was made. It was both untrue and malicious. To thus assail the character of one dead hero over the remains of another was a desecration of the sanctuary; and as far as possible removed from the spirit of charity and magnanimity that are supposed to mark the words of the teacher of the Christian religion.

The sequel showed that the available fighting strength of the hostiles was greater than, or at least fully equal to that of the three columns operating against them combined. As we have seen, Terry, Crook, and Gibbon altogether did not have over 2,700 officers and men. A low estimate gives the hostiles 2,000 to 2,500.[84] There has doubtless been much exaggeration and guess work in the published accounts, but there is little doubt that when Custer went into the fight with his 600 troopers more or less of the Seventh Cavalry he was outnumbered three or four to one. The hostiles were concentrated in one place. They were armed with Winchester rifles and had plenty of fixed ammunition. They were splendid horsemen and well mounted. Custer knew all these things as no other officer knew them, and it is not strange that his face wore a serious expression and that, during much of the time on that last fateful march, he appeared to be in thoughtful and abstracted mood.

Crook's column starting in May marched by way of Old Fort Reno on the Powder River to the headwaters of the Rosebud where, on June 17, he encountered the hostiles and was so badly worsted in a fight with them as to be practically eliminated from the campaign.[85] The fatuous character of the plan of campaign is shown by the fact that, on the day when Crook was waging this unsuccessful battle, Major Reno[86] with a battalion of the Seventh Cavalry was scouting up the Rosebud and, although they were less than fifty miles apart, neither knew of the presence of the other on that river. The Indians were between them. Nor did Terry know of Crook's defeat until long afterwards. Reno's scout, however, disclosed the whereabouts of the hostiles.[87] He discovered their trail and it was correctly assumed that it led to the country along the Little Big Horn.[88]

They had driven Crook away and were preparing to meet the other columns successively as they might appear. But of this Terry knew nothing. He decided to send Custer with his regiment and the Crow and Ree[89] scouts up the Rosebud in pursuit of the Indians whose trail Reno had found. With the remainder of his own and all of Gibbon's command he was to move up the Big Horn to the mouth of the Little Horn, thus preventing the "escape" of the enemy to the north or west, while Custer headed them off to the south and east. In that way was he to circumvent Sitting Bull, the reputed head man of all the hostile Indians.

And here one word as to that redoubtable chief. As a leader of fighting men he was a myth. He had some reputation and influence as a "medicine man" but was in reality a coward and fakir. When Custer attacked the Sioux camp, Sitting Bull took his two wives and his twin children and ran away, not stopping until he was eight or ten miles from the battlefield, to which he did not return until the fighting was over. Then he came back with a flourish and said that he had been in the mountains "propitiating the evil spirits and invoking the gods of war." The real leaders of the Indians who defeated Custer were Gall, Crow King, and Crazy Horse.[90] These

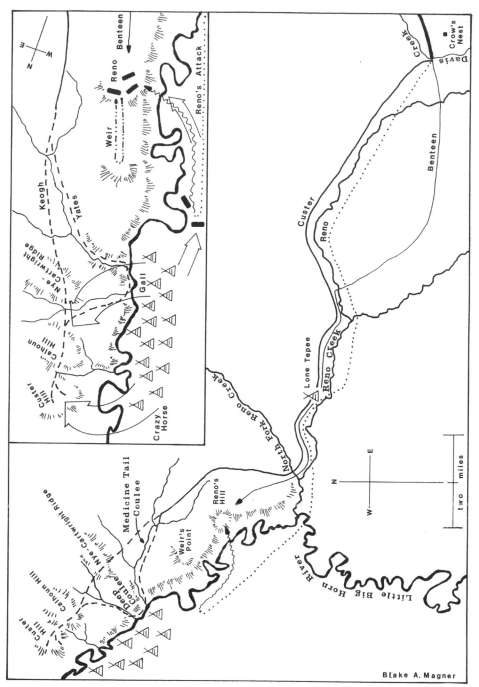

The Battle of Little Big Horn, June 25, 1876

Blake A. Magner

were all Sioux chiefs, though the latter was affiliated with the Cheyennes
through having a Cheyenne woman for his wife. He was chiefly responsible for Crook's defeat and he led the Cheyennes in the battle of the
Little Big Horn.[§] After the battle of June 17, in which Crazy Horse defeated Crook, all the hostiles united under Gall, Sitting Bull "making
medicine" and predicting dire disaster to the whites.

The distance from the mouth of the Rosebud to the camp of the hostiles on the Little Horn was about ninety miles. Custer started on his march
June 22 in the afternoon. He moved twelve miles and encamped. Early in
the evening officers' call summoned the officers to his quarters and a long
conference was held. According to General E. S. Godfrey, who was at that
time lieutenant commanding troop K, of the Seventh, and whose article
published in the *Century Magazine* for January, 1892, is the best account of
the march and battle that has been written, it was not a cheerful meeting.[91]
Custer was plainly depressed. He seemed to defer to the ideas of the other
officers, something very unusual with him. Full instructions were given as
to the details of the march; troop commanders were cautioned to keep
within supporting distance of each other; they were assured that he relied
fully upon their discretion, judgment and loyalty; he explained that he
believed the Seventh Cavalry able to cope successfully with any force it
was likely to meet; and that in his judgment the enemy would not be able
to bring into action more than 1,500 fighting braves at most. His tone was
ingratiating and pleading—so far removed from that which he usually
employed that one of his officers remarked as they were walking away
from the interview:

"Godfrey, I believe that General Custer is going to be killed."

"Why do you think so?" said Godfrey.

"Because I never heard him talk that way before."[**][92]

June 23, starting at five o'clock in the morning and going into camp at
five in the afternoon, the column covered thirty-three miles. The trail of
the Indians became distinct and the pony droppings and other signs indicated a very large party. The scouts were active and vigilant but perturbed,
and the half-breed interpreter[93] predicted that they were going have "a big
fight." Custer rode with the advance and was in constant communication
with the Indian scouts who seemed to become more and more impressed

---

[§]*My Friend the Indian*, by James McLaughlin.
[**]"Custer's Last Battle," by General E. S. Godfrey.

with the magnitude of the task which they had undertaken. The general was habitually grave, reticent and thoughtful.

June 24, the march was slow, painstaking and tedious. The scouts did their work thoroughly and frequent halts were made so as not to get ahead of them. Signs were plentiful and unmistakable. Signal fire smokes were seen. About sundown camp was made after marching twenty-eight miles. This was seventy-three miles from the starting point. At 11:30 the march was resumed and, at 2:00 A.M., the 25th, a halt was made after marching ten miles. Up to this time, it had been the intention of the general to get as near the divide as possible and not cross it until the next night, keeping his command under cover, his plan being to make the attack on the Indian village at daylight, or before daylight on the 26th. At eight o'clock he broke camp and marched till 10:30, making ten miles and secreted his command in a ravine.

While here he seems to have concluded that further attempts at concealment were useless, that the enemy was aware of his approach and that to carry out his orders to prevent their escape it would be necessary to attack the camp at once. He had personally verified the report of the scouts as to the location of the hostiles on the west side of the river, the camp extending some three or four miles along the river from its upper to its lower end. He gave orders to advance to the attack and, soon after starting, divided his regiment into three battalions—one of three troops under Major Reno; one of three troops under Captain Benteen[94]; and one of five troops under his own immediate command. One troop brought up the rear with the pack train which carried the reserve ammunition. Reno had the advance, closely followed by Custer. Benteen was directed to go several hundred yards to the left and "pitch into" anything that he met. In this way the river was approached, opposite the upper end of the village. When Reno arrived pretty close to the river, Custer ordered him to cross, advance as rapidly as he deemed prudent, and when he struck the village to charge it and he would be supported by "the entire outfit." Custer then turned to the right along a ridge parallel with the river with the obvious purpose of attacking the village lower down at the same time that Reno made his charge. Custer's march was within plain sight of the Indian camp, but Reno's approach was unseen and the Indians were taken by surprise. No intimation of danger from that direction had come to the Indians until bullets from Reno's carbines began to whiz through the tepees. This it was that caused the flight of Sitting Bull. Undoubtedly Custer exposed his column to view in order to divert attention from Reno's movement. It is also certain that he expected Reno to obey his order to charge the village, and believed that it would give him (Custer) an opportunity to strike an effective blow lower down. Reno's attack struck terror into the village and, if it had been pressed, as Custer thought it would be, the stampede which Sitting Bull started might have become general. But, unfortunately, it was not pressed. Reno headed a stampede back across the river into the hills. Gall and the fighting braves who had hurried from the lower end of the camp, where they had been watching Custer, to meet Reno's unexpected attack, after following him across the river had time to return to the lower end and take part in the destruction of Custer and his battalion. They even used the guns and ammunition and rode the horses which they had captured from Reno in his retreat. Reno's ignominious retreat allowed the entire force of hostiles to concentrate in front of Custer.[95] When Gall, after driving Reno to the hills, returned to the lower end of the camp where Crazy Horse was with the Cheyennes, Custer's column was still some distance away. Reno had as much time to go to Custer's relief as Gall had to return and get into the fight with Custer, but he does not appear to have had a thought of going to the aid of his chief.

The last that was seen of Custer alive was when Reno after crossing the river was advancing toward the Indian village. He waved his hat as if to encourage Reno and his men, a cheer was heard and then he moved on to do his part. The trail and the accounts given by the Indians show that he did not swerve from his purpose to attack the Indian camp until he was overwhelmed by the combined force of the hostiles all concentrated against the five troops which went to death with him.

At the time when Custer was seen to wave his hat and his men were heard to cheer, he seems to have begun to realize, if he had not suspected it before, that the hostile force was greater than even he had estimated, for an order written by Cook,[96] the adjutant, was dispatched by a trumpeter to Benteen which read as follows:

"Benteen, come on, big village. Be quick. Bring packs. P.S. Bring packs."

The imperative nature of the order is apparent at a glance.

"Come on! Be quick! Big village! Bring packs! Bring packs!" could have but one meaning. Benteen was needed. The necessity of having the reserve ammunition on hand had become apparent. Reno was attacking the village and Custer was going to support the attack by assailing it lower down, but he wanted Benteen with his three troops and the pack train and

its one troop and its ammunition, making four troops in all, which would
very nearly double the force which he had with him. Besides, it was essential that Benteen be brought into the engagement in order to support
Reno with "the whole outfit" as he had promised. He had no reason to
doubt that Benteen when he received that order would certainly "Come
on" and "Be quick" about it. Also, he had no reason to doubt that Reno
would hold the attention of the hostiles, who were not numerous in his
front, until Custer reinforced by Benteen could reach the point of attack
toward which they were moving. Benteen had plenty of time to overtake
Custer if he had zealously and in good faith obeyed the order to "Come
on!" and "Be quick!" The trumpeter who brought the order went back
and was killed with the others. Custer's march was slow. He was clearly
looking for Benteen to join him before making the attack. If he suspected
that Reno had been driven back, he had a right to suppose that both Reno
and Benteen would make the effort to come to his aid, for he could see
that the Indians were concentrating in his own front. Disappointed in this,
he must have concluded that it was his duty to go ahead and support Reno
"with the whole outfit" as he had promised, perilous as he must have
deemed it to do this with his small force. He doubtless waited till all hope
of help was lost and then with a brave heart went to his death.

Reno disobeyed his orders when he failed to charge the village. If he
had done that, it is the testimony of the Indians who were there, says
McLaughlin,[97] that he would have thrown it into such a state of conster-
nation at the time when Sitting Bull ran away that the diversion would
have materially aided Custer's movement. If Reno had not stampeded to
the hills on the other side of the river, Benteen would have obeyed his
order to "Come on" and "Be quick." He would have overtaken Custer and
the result might have been different. Reno ran away to the hills without
making any fight at all, to speak of. Benteen came up, found him there and
was ordered to remain with him.[98] That was at 2:30. Custer was not defeated till 3 o'clock. After Benteen joined Reno, two distinct volleys were
heard in the direction where Custer was. Godfrey's opinion is that they
were fired as signals. Who will say that, if Reno had taken up the march
immediately with the seven troops that he had with him, in the direction
of the sound of that firing, there would not have been a different story to
tell of the battle of the Little Big Horn.

The result is known. General Sherman said that when he came in con-
tact with the Indians Custer had no alternative but to fight. His orders
from General Terry contemplated that he should go out in "pursuit" of

the Indians and prevent their "escape." Nothing could be plainer or more explicit than those orders. Everything else was left to Custer's judgment. "Do not allow them to escape by passing to the southeast around your left flank" was the sum and substance of those final orders. It was for this purpose, of course, that Benteen's battalion was sent out on the left flank, but when it was found that the Indians, so far from retreating and trying to escape were in reality waiting for a fight, the necessity for this flanking movement was at an end. Benteen was called in by a peremptory order which read: "Benteen, come on! Be quick! Big village! Bring packs! Bring packs!" The very wording of the order indicates its urgency. When Custer went to the high point overlooking the valley where the Sioux and their allies were encamped he saw that it was a "big village"—much bigger than he or anybody else had foreseen—that the Indians were not running away; that immense herds of ponies were grazing in the distance; that the hostiles were on the alert and awaiting his approach; he would not turn back. He must go on and support Reno with the whole outfit, Benteen included.

But, what of Benteen? He had not yet come into the fight. "Come on! Benteen! Be quick! Bring packs! Bring packs! Big village!"

Halting only long enough to dictate this earnest and urgent appeal—this positive order—which from any officer receiving it demanded instant obedience; and which any soldier of the heroic mold would die rather than to disobey; and resting in the assurance that it would be obeyed, Custer went on to his duty and his doom.[99]

The despatch was received by the officer to whom it was sent. It was placed in the hands of Captain Benteen. It reached its destination in time. But Benteen did not come. He found Reno cowering in the hills and reported to him. Both of these officers, after their junction, heard the volleys fired as signals for them to "come on" and "be quick." They heard but did not heed. And while they hesitated Custer and his little band of heroes were done to death. Not a single one escaped to tell the story of how it was done.

Two days later Terry with Gibbon's column came up from the north and west. The Indians had escaped around Gibbon's flank. Reno and Benteen were there. They had saved their lives, but Custer and two hundred and sixteen of his officers and men lay dead, naked and mutilated on the field where they fought.[100] Custer and Captain Keogh were the only ones who escaped mutilation after death.[101]

Thus died our hero. A modest stone erected by the government marks the spot where he fell. His remains, easily identified, were removed and interred at West Point on the Hudson, a fitting place of sepulture for one who never failed in his duty to his country, his family or to his own manhood. "May he rest in peace" and may his memory ever be kept green is the wish of every survivor of those who fought under him and knew his sterling worth as a solder and as a man.[††]

NOTES

1. Custer died at the Little Big Horn on June 26, 1876.

2. Prince Rupert, Count Palatine of the Rhine, Duke of Bavaria (1619–1682), Anglo-German general and admiral who served with great competence in the Thirty Years War, English Civil War, and many other conflicts. He was appointed commander of the cavalry of King Charles I of England in the English Civil War. He was a brave and brilliant cavalry commander.

3. Joachim Murat, King of Naples, Duke of Cleve and Berg (1767–1815), French Marshal of the Empire and Grand Admiral of the Empire. Murat was chief of cavalry under Napoleon I, emperor of France. As a commander of horse, he had few peers. He was later executed by firing squad when his attempts to regain his throne were rebuffed. Napoleon wrote of Murat that he was "the bravest of men in the face of the enemy, incomparable on the battlefield, but a fool in his actions everywhere else."

4. Maj. Gen. James Ewell Brown Stuart, commander of Gen. Robert E. Lee's Confederate Cavalry Division.

5. King George III, ruler of Great Britain in the late eighteenth century, hired Hessian mercenaries to fight for him during the Revolutionary War.

6. Thomas Ward Custer, born on March 15, 1845.

7. Custer's mother was his father's second wife. Born Maria Ward in 1807, she was married to Israel Kirkpatrick at the age of sixteen. After fathering three children, Kirkpatrick died in 1835, a year after the first Mrs. Custer. Maria Kirkpatrick married Emmanuel Custer on April 14, 1837, and the couple had five children together, with George Armstrong Custer born in 1839. Frederick Whittaker, *A Complete Life of General George A. Custer*, 2 vols. (New York: Sheldon, 1876), 1:4.

8. Lydia A. Kirkpatrick, Custer's half-sister, married David A. Reed of Monroe.

[††]An article by General Nelson A. Miles in the Cosmopolitan Magazine for June 1911, which came to hand when I was reading the proof of the foregoing, intimates that Gall and his force of Indians, after driving Reno to the hills did not cross the river but followed Custer's trail, thus placing themselves between Reno and Custer on the same side, attacking Custer's rear and left flank when Crazy Horse and the others, crossing the river lower down, came in on his front and right flank.

This makes it all the worse for Reno and Benteen. If they had advanced when the volleys were fired after their junction this would have prevented Gall's successful attack on Custer. Fifteen minutes would have brought them into the action.—J. H. K.

9. Ironically, Custer's nephew, Autie Reed, would die with him at the Battle of Little Big Horn on June 25, 1876.

10. Nevin J. Custer, born July 29, 1842.

11. In fact, George A. Custer was also a life-long Democrat. In the years immediately following the end of the Civil War, when the Republicans dominated the American political scene, Custer loyally followed the lead of the Republicans, running afoul of Republican president U. S. Grant, an error in judgment that significantly impeded the progress of Custer's military career, and which explains why he received no promotions in the ten years from Custer's appointment as lieutenant colonel of the 7th Cavalry until his death.

12. Jefferson Davis, a Mississippian and hero of the Mexican War, served as secretary of war during the administration of President James Buchanan, 1856–60. Davis served as the only president of the Confederacy.

13. Lt. Col. John F. Reynolds, of Lancaster, Pennsylvania. A member of the West Point class of 1841, Reynolds was an accomplished artillerist who would be offered command of the Union's Army of the Potomac in the days just prior to the Battle of Gettysburg. Reynolds was killed during the morning phase of the fighting on the first day of that battle.

14. Robert E. Lee's nephew, Lt. Fitzhugh Lee, a member of West Point's Class of 1852. Lee later achieved the rank of major general in his uncle's Army of Northern Virginia and commanded a division of cavalry therein.

15. This refers to Pierce Manning Butler Young.

16. This comes from Custer's unfinished memoir of his military service in the Civil War. Those portions that were completed were serialized in *Galaxy Magazine*. Modern historian John M. Carroll collected those chapters, as well as other of Custer's writings, in a volume titled *Custer in the Civil War: His Unfinished Memoirs* (San Rafael, Calif.: Presidio Press, 1977). (Quote on p. 87.)

17. Brig. Gen. Irvin McDowell, a member of the West Point class of 1834, was considered to be a great scholar of Napoleonic tactics and was given tactical command of the newly formed Union volunteer army assigned to the defenses of Washington.

18. Maj. Gen. Philip Kearny of New York, nephew of the legendary dragoon officer Brig. Gen. Stephen Watts Kearny and heir to a large fortune. Kearny, a dashing cavalryman who lost an arm in battle during the Mexican War, was killed in action at the Battle of Chantilly, Virginia, on September 1, 1862.

19. Maj. Gen. William Farrar Smith, a member of West Point's class of 1841, was decorated a number of times for gallant and meritorious service during the Civil War.

20. Maj. Gen. Winfield Scott Hancock, a member of West Point's class of 1840, was one of the finest officers of the Civil War.

21. Brig. Gen. John G. Bernard, a member of West Point's class of 1829.

22. McClellan, a member of the West Point class of 1846, was the Army of the Potomac's first commander. Later the Democratic presidential nominee in 1864, McClellan was one of the many high ranking officers to lend a hand in Custer's mercurial rise to high command during the Civil War.

23. Maj. Gen. Ambrose E. Burnside, a member of West Point's class of 1846, commanded the Army of the Potomac from November 1862 to February 1863.

24. Austin Blair, wartime governor of Michigan.

25. Custer petitioned to be appointed colonel of the newly formed 5th Michigan Cavalry, a petition that was rejected. Instead, Russell Alger, a politically connected lawyer, received the appointment. Alger commanded the regiment for the balance of the war. He later served as secretary of war during William McKinley's presidency and held the post during the Spanish-American War.

26. Brig. Gen. John Buford, of Kentucky, a member of West Point's class of 1848. Generally considered to be the finest cavalry officer in Federal service, Buford died of typhoid fever on December 16, 1863. He and Custer are buried a few yards apart in the cemetery at the Military Academy at West Point.

27. Brig. Gen. Alfred Pleasonton, of West Point's class of 1840, was another career cavalryman. Pleasonton became Custer's patron and most ardent supporter. They grew to have an extremely close relationship, much like a father and son. Custer owed much of his military reputation and success to the support of Pleasonton.

28. This severe fight, on June 17, 1863, was an important engagement during the Confederate advance into Pennsylvania in the days just prior to the Battle of Gettysburg.

29. Col. (later Maj. Gen.) Hugh Judson Kilpatrick, a member of West Point's class of 1856, was promoted to division command a few days before Custer was promoted to brigade command in June 1863.

30. Col. Calvin Douty, commander of the 1st Maine Cavalry.

31. Brig. Gen. Elon J. Farnsworth, the nephew of Pleasonton's political patron, the influential Illinois congressman John F. Farnsworth. Formerly one of Pleasonton's staff officers, Elon Farnsworth was promoted directly from captain to brigadier general of volunteers on the same day as Custer. Unfortunately, Farnsworth would be killed leading a futile mounted charge against Confederate infantry in a foolhardy counterattack ordered by Kilpatrick in the wake of the repulse of Pickett's Charge at Gettysburg on July 3, 1863. For more on Farnsworth's heroic charge and death, see Eric J. Wittenberg, *Gettysburg's Forgotten Cavalry Actions* (Gettysburg, Pa.: Thomas Publications, 1998).

32. Col. Thornton Fleming Brodhead was breveted for gallant and meritorious service in the Mexican War. At the outbreak of the war, Brodhead was appointed to command the 1st Michigan Cavalry. He was mortally wounded in a wild cavalry melee at the Lewis Ford in the closing engagement of the Second Battle of Bull Run, August 30, 1862.

33. Maj. Gen. Joseph Hooker, a member of West Point's class of 1833, known as "Fighting Joe," commanded the Army of the Potomac from February to June 28, 1863.

34. The brigades of Brig. Gens. Wade Hampton and Fitzhugh Lee and the brigade of Col. John Chambliss, commanding the brigade of Brig. Gen. William H. F. "Rooney" Lee, who had been severely wounded at the Battle of Brandy Station on June 9, 1863, and then captured by the advancing Federals a few days later. Rooney Lee was a son of Robert E. Lee.

35. King Henry IV of France (1533–1610) was especially adept at using his cavalry and lancers to good effect and was also a brilliant field general.

36. This was Kidd's dear friend Henry E. Thompson, who preceded Kidd in command of the 6th Michigan Cavalry and who later received a brevet to brigadier general of volunteers for his gallant and meritorious service in the Civil War.

37. Kidd refers to Lt. Alexander C. M. Pennington, a member of West Point's class of 1855, who eventually achieved the rank of brigadier general in the Regular Army. One of the finest artillerists of the nineteeth century, Pennington also briefly commanded a brigade of cavalry under Custer.

38. Brig. Gen. Charles King, a member of West Point's class of 1862.

39. Brig. Gen. Wesley Merritt, a member of West Point's class of 1860, was also promoted to brigadier general of volunteers on June 28, 1863. One of the finest cavalry officers ever produced, Merritt served in the Regular Army for forty-three years, served as commandant of the Military Academy at West Point, distinguished himself as an Indian fighter, and later commanded the expedition that captured Manila during the Spanish-American War. When he finally retired, Merritt was a major general in the Regular Army. He was also buried in the cemetery at West Point, a few yards from Custer. For nearly their entire careers, Custer and Merritt had a healthy rivalry, although Merritt ultimately accomplished more than his younger rival. Ironically, Merritt commanded the expedition to punish the Sioux Indians in the aftermath of the massacre of the 7th Cavalry at the Battle of Little Big Horn.

40. Bvt. Maj. Gen. Thomas C. Devin of New York. Devin, much older than the other cavalry commanders of the Army of the Potomac, was not a West Pointer. Rather, he had served for many years in the New York militia and earned the respect of all who served with him. He had two nicknames, "Buford's Hard Hitter" or "Old Warhorse." Buford once said of him, "I can't teach Col. Devin anything about cavalry—he knows more than I do." At the conclusion of the Civil War, Devin served as lieutenant colonel of the 8th Cavalry and colonel of the 3d Cavalry before dying in 1878. He was also buried in the cemetery at West Point.

41. Each of these engagements was fought during the retreat from Gettysburg. Kidd was badly wounded in the foot at the battle of Falling Waters on July 13, 1863.

42. The two rival armies ended up back where they had begun the spring campaigning season, staring each other down along the opposite banks of the Rappahannock River. Along the way, there were a number of bitter and bloody fights between the two armies.

43. Judge Daniel S. Bacon.

44. Known as the Kilpatrick-Dahlgren Raid, this expedition was a disaster. The raid was commanded jointly by Kilpatrick and a promising young cavalryman named Col. Ulric Dahlgren. Intended to dash into Richmond and free Union prisoners of war held in Libby Prison and on Belle Isle, the raid instead was a disaster that cost Dahlgren his life.

45. Custer took a select group of five hundred officers and men of the Reserve Brigade on a diversionary raid into Albemarle County, with the destruction of the Virginia Central Railroad in the area of Charlottesville as its mission. Unlike the Kilpatrick-Dahlgren Raid, this expedition was successful.

46. Brig. Gen. David McM. Gregg, a member of West Point's class of 1851, commanded the Second Division of the Army of the Potomac's Cavalry Corps.

47. One of Custer's troopers, perhaps John Huff of the 5th Michigan Cavalry, inflicted a mortal wound on Stuart during one of the hard-fought, close melees during the Battle of Yellow Tavern.

48. Maj. Gen. Philip H. Sheridan, appointed to replace Pleasonton as commander of the Cavalry Corps in April 1864.

49. A brigade of North Carolina cavalry commanded by Brig. Gen. James B. Gordon, who was killed in combat in the summer of 1864.

50. Brig. Gen. Rufus Barringer of the 1st North Carolina Cavalry.

51. This was a fine brigade of South Carolina mounted infantry commanded by Brig. Gen. Matthew C. Butler, a protégé of Wade Hampton. Butler had a foot taken off by a Federal artillery shell at Stevensburg during the Battle of Brandy Station on June 9, 1863. Butler eventually achieved the rank of major general and commanded a division of Confederate cavalry in late 1864 and through the end of the war. After the war, Butler became a prominent politician in South Carolina.

52. James Thomas Brudenel, the 7th Earl of Cardigan (1797–1868), who as a major general commanded the Light Cavalry Brigade in Lord Lucan's cavalry division, is the officer who gave the order for the immortal charge of the Light Brigade.

53. At the decisive moment of the Battle of Balaklava on October 25, 1854, during the Crimean War, the British Light Cavalry Brigade made a hopeless saber charge against Russian artillery and infantry in place. Of the six hundred men who made the charge, more than half did not return. The charge of the British horse was immortalized in Tennyson's epic poem "The Charge of the Light Brigade."

54. The Reserve Brigade consisted of the 1st, 2d, and 5th U.S. Cavalry; the 6th Pennsylvania Cavalry; and the 1st New York Dragoons. It was a fine brigade that often had the most difficult tasks asked of the Federal cavalry during the first two years of the Civil War.

55. Maj. Gen. David Hunter, who commanded a Federal army assigned to capture and destroy the Shenandoah Valley, was repulsed by the Confederates at Lynchburg later in June.

56. Brig. Gen. Alfred T. A. Torbert, a member of the West Point class of 1855, originally served in the infantry and competently commanded a brigade of New Jersey infantry in 1862 and 1863. A West Point friend of Sheridan's, Torbert was given command of the Army of the Potomac's First Cavalry Division in the spring of 1864, even though he had never served with or commanded cavalry prior to his appointment.

57. The brigades of Hampton, Butler, Rosser, Fitz Lee, and P. M. B. Young.

58. Maj. Gen. John C. Breckinridge, of Kentucky, had served as vice president of the United States in the Buchanan administration. With the coming of war, Breckinridge cast his lot with the Confederacy and, despite his lack of military training, proved himself a competent commander of infantry. In the spring of 1865 he accepted an appointment as the Confederacy's last secretary of war. After the war, he returned home to Kentucky.

59. Brig. Gen. Thomas L. Rosser's Laurel Brigade, consisting of the 7th, 11th, and 12th Regiments of Virginia Cavalry and the 35th Battalion of Virginia Cavalry. This was, perhaps, the finest Confederate cavalry brigade. Rosser, of course, was Custer's West Point classmate and close friend. After the end of the war, they would resume their friendship.

60. This is precisely the circumstance that Custer found himself in at the Battle of Little Big Horn on June 25, 1876. Fortunately for Custer, his legendary luck held at Trevilian Station, and reinforcements made their way to his rescue this day.

61. Rosser was wounded in the leg that day.

62. Kidd misquotes Grant's order to Maj. Gen. David Hunter. Grant actually ordered Hunter's troops "to eat out Virginia clear and clean as far as they go, so that crows flying over

it for the balance of the season will have to carry their provender with them." *OR*, vol. 43, 2:366. For a detailed study of the destruction of the Shenandoah Valley, known as "The Burning," see John L. Heatwole, *The Burning: Sheridan in the Shenandoah Valley* (Lexington, Va.: Rockbridge Publishing, 1998).

63. Maj. Gen. Richard H. Anderson's Confederate division.

64. This is Shepherdstown Ford, located in West Virginia near the Antietam battlefield.

65. Brig. Gen. William W. Averell, also a member of West Point's class of 1855, was colonel of the 3d Pennsylvania Cavalry early in the war. He was promoted to brigadier general of volunteers in 1862 and commanded a brigade of cavalry in 1863. However, his poor performance during the Stoneman Raid, during the Chancellorsville campaign, April–May 1863, led to his relief. At the time that the Army of the Shenandoah was formed in the summer of 1864, Averell was the senior Union cavalry commander in the Valley. As a result of his timid performance, he would be relieved of command by Sheridan in the fall of 1864, an episode that traumatized Averell.

66. Brig. Gen. James H. Wilson, a member of West Point's class of 1860, Wilson was another of Custer's great rivals. Custer despised Wilson and felt that he was not competent for the high level of command that he reached. However, Wilson was a great favorite of Lt. Gen. Ulysses S. Grant and was appointed to high command as a result of that close relationship. Wilson proved himself incompetent, however, and was exiled to the Western Theater, where he succeeded in inflicting one of the few defeats that Lt. Gen. Nathan B. Forrest suffered in the Civil War. Wilson had a long career in the Regular Army and became a prolific writer later in his life.

67. Maj. Gen. William T. Sherman, commander of all Union troops in the Western Theater and Grant's principal lieutenant.

68. Brig. Gen. Henry E. Davies, originally of the 2d New York Cavalry, who commanded a brigade of Union cavalry in Gregg's Division.

69. In the Battle of Tom's Brook, October 8, 1864, also known as the Woodstock Races, the Union cavalry inflicted the war's worst defeat on its grayclad counterparts. Driven from the field in a wild rout, the Yankee cavalry pursued the beaten Confederates for twenty-six miles before giving up the chase.

70. The Battle of Waynesborough, fought on March 1, 1865, marked the end of the fighting career of Lt. Gen. Jubal A. Early and his Army of the Valley. Commanding the Federal cavalry in a grand charge, Custer's troopers destroyed the remnant of Early's army there. For more information on the Battle of Waynesborough, see Harlan Lloyd Page, "The Battle of Waynesborough." in Paul Andrew Hutton, ed., *The Custer Reader* (Lincoln: University of Nebraska Press, 1992), 69–82.

71. Lee surrendered the Army of Northern Virginia at Appomattox Court House on April 9, 1865. Custer personally received the flag of truce.

72. The last fight between the Federal and Confederate cavalry took place at Sailor's Creek on April 6, 1865. Custer's brother, Lt. Thomas Custer, was awarded the Medal of Honor for capturing a Confederate battle flag at Sailor's Creek.

73. The critical engagement during the breakout from the siege lines at Petersburg occurred when Sheridan launched an attack on the Confederate lines at the critical road junction

at Five Forks, to the west of Petersburg. This fight, which took place on April 1, 1865, led to Lee's abandonment of Petersburg and began the retreat west, away from Petersburg.

74. Actually, Custer was not appointed lieutenant colonel of the newly formed 7th Cavalry in June 1866. Until that time, he reverted to his Regular Army rank of captain after serving in Texas. The 7th Cavalry was generally considered to be an elite regiment, given the specific task of fighting Indians on the western frontier.

75. Col. Samuel E. Sturgis, nominal commander of the regiment, almost never served in the field with his command, usually leaving tactical command to Custer.

76. Kidd refers here to Custer's success at the Battle of Washita, wherein he commanded a column that included the 7th Cavalry and some Kansas volunteers against Cheyenne Indians. On November 23, 1868, Custer launched a surprise attack on a large Indian village. Dividing his column, sending one column directly into the village and a second column on a flanking movement, Custer inflicted a crushing defeat on the Indians, including the death of their chief, Black Kettle. This battle established Custer as a leading Indian fighter and established the tactics that he would later repeat at the Battle of the Little Big Horn in June 1876. For a detailed study of Custer's Washita Campaign, see Stan Hoig, *The Battle of the Washita* (Lincoln: University of Nebraska Press, 1976); and Hutton, *The Custer Reader*. Custer's success in the engagement at Washita led to his belief in launching direct attacks on large Indian villages. It also created a great deal of dissension within the ranks of the 7th Cavalry. His second in command, Maj. Joel Elliott, was killed in the action, and Custer left his body behind, instead of bringing it out. This action caused a great deal of resentment against Custer among the regiment's officers, many of whom never forgave him. One of those disgruntled officers was Capt. Frederick Benteen.

77. This is not as clear-cut an issue as Kidd would lead the reader to believe. A number of officers could legitimately claim that title, including, but not limited to, Custer.

78. Sheridan, commanding general of the army, authorized the campaign. The strategy for the campaign was to launch converging columns on the large Indian encampment known to be in the "unceded lands" in the region of the Powder River. Most of the Indians involved were Sioux, but members of other tribes were also involved. The campaign stemmed from the Federal government's attempts to make the Black Hills area of the Montana territory available for gold prospecting and the Indians' refusal to open their lands to white development. All involved, including the department commander, Gen. Alfred H. Terry, believed that the Sioux Indians that were the target of the campaign would attempt to escape from the converging army columns. For one of the better studies of the 1876 Sioux campaign, see John S. Gray, *Centennial Campaign: The Sioux War of 1876* (Norman: University of Oklahoma Press, 1988); and Edgar I. Stewart, *Custer's Luck* (Norman: University of Oklahoma Press, 1955).

79. Brig. Gen. John Gibbon, a member of the West Point class of 1847 and a major hero of the Civil War.

80. Brig. Gen. George Crook, a member of the West Point class of 1852, was the last commander of the Army of the Potomac's Cavalry Corps. Crook had a lofty reputation as an Indian fighter and later brought Geronimo to bay.

81. Brig. Gen. Alfred H. Terry, originally of the 2d Connecticut Infantry, was not a West Pointer. Despite that fact, he eventually reached the rank of major general in the Regular Army.

82. In reality, there were probably fewer than six hundred officers and men on the expedition.

83. This is probably Lt. Col. Martin B. Hughes of the 9th Cavalry.

84. The size of the Indian village and strength of the Indian force has been a subject of dispute for many years. Recent scholarship indicates that there may have been as many as seven thousand Indians in the village and as many as two thousand warriors involved in the Battle of the Little Big Horn. See Robert M. Utley, "The Little Big Horn," in Hutton, *The Custer Reader*, 248.

85. On June 2, 1876, Crook's column set out to march up the valley of the Rosebud River. Nearly two weeks into their march, they found evidence of Indian hunting parties. Setting out to pursue the hostiles, Crook ran into a large party of Sioux and Cheyenne warriors along the banks of the Rosebud on June 17. Crook was defeated in this engagement, suffering nine killed and twenty-three wounded. Crook then withdrew and gave up the pursuit of the Indians. For more on the Battle of the Rosebud, see Gray, *Centennial Campaign*, 110–24.

86. Maj. Marcus A. Reno, who received a brevet to brigadier general of volunteers in the Civil War, was Custer's second in command when the 7th Cavalry took the field in June 1876. He would be court-martialed and cashiered from the army for his role in the Battle of the Little Big Horn.

87. Kidd refers to Reno's senior Ree scout, Forked Horn.

88. Kidd himself briefly served as an Indian fighter in the months immediately following the end of the Civil War when the Michigan Cavalry Brigade was sent west to the Powder River country to fight the Sioux. Kidd himself traversed some of the terrain covered by Custer's expedition and likely remembered it well from his brief stint as a reluctant Indian fighter.

89. There were a number of Indian bands allied with the Federal government in their enmity of the Sioux, including the Crows and Rees.

90. While the Indians had no command hierarchy, Crazy Horse and Gall seemed to have been their principal leaders in the combat.

91. Kidd refers to Edward S. Godfrey, whose article "Custer's Last Battle" is considered one of the classic accounts of the disaster that befell Custer on the Little Big Horn. The article Kidd mentions appears verbatim in Hutton, *The Custer Reader*.

92. This exchange may be found in Hutton, *The Custer Reader*, 277.

93. This is probably Mitch Bouyer, half-French and half-Sioux, who served as Custer's main guide on the advance.

94. Capt. Frederick Benteen, a brave and experienced troop commander, despised Custer, in part as a result of the controversy surrounding Maj. Elliott's death at the Battle of Washita. Some would blame Benteen's personal animosity toward Custer for his failure to reinforce Custer's column at the Battle of the Little Big Horn, thereby dooming Custer and his men to death.

95. Reno seemed to freeze under fire, and some have accused him of being intoxicated while in command of his column at the Little Big Horn. A strong Indian counterattack drove his column back from the village, which probably saved Reno's entire column from slaughter. The village was so large, and so many warriors were seen, that Reno pulled up short of the village instead of pitching into it, thereby allowing most of his column to escape to safety. Reno did not act to go the aid of Custer, and he also seems to have done little to save his own

command. He was later court-martialed for his conduct that day and was cashiered from the army in disgrace.

96. Lt. William W. Cooke, regimental adjutant, died with Custer on Custer Hill.

97. This refers to James McLaughlin, who wrote a book titled *My Friend the Indian* (Boston: Houghton-Mifflin Co., 1910), an account of the campaign from the perspective of the Indians.

98. To his credit, when Benteen found Reno seemingly paralyzed by fear, he took command of their combined force and, through his own courage and good leadership, saved what was left of the 7th Cavalry.

99. Custer chose a high ridge to make his famous "last stand." Surrounded by his officers and approximately forty enlisted men, including his brother, Capt. Thomas Custer, Custer drew his little force up into a circle and resisted the Indians as long as they could. The overwhelming numbers of the enemy gradually wore the brave little band of horse soldiers down, until none was left alive. After the fight, many of the Indians praised the bravery of the men of the 7th Cavalry, singling out Custer in particular for his courage.

100. Kidd understates the number of casualties. The actual numbers were 16 officers and 237 enlisted men killed, for total dead of 253. See Gray, *Centennial Campaign*, 289.

101. Most of the bodies of the troopers of the 7th Cavalry were mutilated by the women of the Indian village after the fighting ended. Kate Big Head, a Cheyenne woman who witnessed the fighting, later recounted that Custer's body was saved from mutilation by the Cheyennes, who had known him in the southern campaigns in the years immediately after the Civil War. Kate Big Head reported that only one of his fingers were cut off and that sewing awls were placed in Custer's ears "to improve his hearing." See Kate Big Head, "She Watched Custer's Last Battle," in Hutton, *The Custer Reader*, 376. Capt. Myles W. Keogh, commander of Troop G, died with his command on a low ridge near the location of Custer's last stand. Keogh, who wore a large papal medal around his neck as a result of his service in the Papal Wars in Italy in the years just before the Civil War, was also spared mutilation, probably as a result of the medal. See John P. Langellier, Kurt Hamilton Cox, and Brian C. Pohanka, eds., *Myles Keogh: The Life and Legend of an "Irish Dragoon" in the Seventh Cavalry* (El Segundo, Calif.: Upton and Sons, 1998), 156.

Appendix A
Operations of Our Cavalry:
The Michigan Cavalry Brigade

by E. A. Paul, New York Times, *August 6, 1863*

Headquarters Army of the Potomac
Sunday, Aug. 2

The miscarriage of several letters intended for the *Times*, giving accounts of recent cavalry movements, renders a brief resume of their contents necessary.

When marching into Maryland and Pennsylvania, the spirits of the Union troops were buoyant, because they felt that the enemy had placed himself in a position from which it would be impossible to escape without loss of all his materials of war. This accomplished, the war would be practically at an end. How bitterly all were disappointed need not be repeated here. There were not wanting those who professed to believe that this disappointment would tend greatly to demoralize the army, and in such an extent as to undermine all further aggressive operations until a reorganization could be effected. But how different the result? When the order was given to recross the Potomac, the troops moved forward as cheerfully as ever, cracking jokes and singing their marching songs—the most common being the very ones prohibited eighteen months ago by their commanding General, whose stars are now somewhat obscured. Remaining a day behind at Boonsboro, and crossing at Berlin, on my way to the cavalry command at Snicker's Gap, I passed on the road in two days all of the infantry organizations. It was exceedingly agreeable to find the troops again so cheerful, greeting "Old Dixie" familiarly, and pointing out, as they went along, localities well known to most of them—every town, village and city having its history with some portion of the army.

The cavalry recrossed the Potomac at different points. That under Gen. Gregg harassed the rear of the enemy, while Buford, Custer, and Merritt operated upon their left flank and "interior lines," doing the double duty of annoying the enemy on his flank and at the same time protecting their our immense wagon trains from the raids of bushwhackers, who are to be found everywhere in Virginia. This will always be the case until the Burnside policy is adopted—permitting no man to stray within our lines unless he takes the oath of allegiance. The futile attempts to hold Mosby and his sixty men in check has probably cost the Government, during the last year, quite as much as any single army corps, and still Mosby's band was as active and destructive today as it was one year ago. The reason of this is quite plain to those familiar with this beat. While he has nominally a small force, no matter how many men he may lose, his command is always full, and then all the male white population of Northeastern Virginia cooperate with him. Citizens do picket duty, act as spies, and a greater or less number of farmers in every neighborhood always have horses ready saddled, and Mosby is regularly informed of every movement made by any body of Union troops, and they also stand ready to take a hand whenever a fight is the order of the day. When any of these citizen soldiers are called to an account, they are equally ready to make oath that they have done nothing to aid Mosby—a majority of them believing such oath not to be binding.

Full justice, as I have already said, in many instances, has been rendered to regiments, and sometimes whole brigades of our cavalry force. The service of which deserve more than a passing notice of the troops thus neglected are the four regiments-First, Fifth, Sixth and Seventh—known as the Michigan brigade, at present commanded by Col. Town of the First—formerly by Gen. Custer. These regiments, taken as a whole, will compare favorably with any cavalry regiments. The officers and men for the most part are those who, by entering the service, made large sacrifices, and who were prompted to the step by as patriotic motives as ever inspired the breast of a true lover of his country. Soldiering with them is not a pastime, a spree, a holiday, but a duty, and men thus animated, whatever they to do is done well.

How such men can dies is illustrated by following incidents: After the fight had closed on the right at Gettysburgh—Friday night, July 3—Lieut. Barse found his brother, Corp. H. S. Barse, of Company E, Fifth Michigan Cavalry, upon the field, wounded in the abdomen. He had him conveyed to the hospital, where Dr. Wooster pronounced the wound a mortal one. Lieut.

Barse communicated the intelligence to his brother who, to his surprise, manifested no great emotion. A moment afterward he asked his brother if he desired to send any word through him to their parents, as his duties would require him to leave with his regiment at once. The dying boy raised his eyes calmly until he met the agonized gaze of his brother, and looking at him steadily for moment said, "Yes. Tell Father and Mother that I died doing my duty in a noble cause, and that I contented." The Lieutenant, a soon as he could regain sufficient composure, knowing that his brother was much attached to a young lady, asked him, "Do you wish to send anything to any one else?" "Yes," he replied, "tell Emily the same," and the brothers parted never to meet again this side of the grave. I cannot refrain here from relating a circumstance in connection with this case, reflecting great credit upon one citizen of Pennsylvania, at least. After the rebel army had re-crossed the Potomac, Lieut. Barse obtained permission to take his brother's body to Detroit. Visiting Gettysburgh, the lowest price for which any person would carry himself and the remains of his brother thirty miles, to a railroad depot, was Sixty Dollars, a sum which he actually paid.

I have space to-day for one more incident of many that have come under my own observation. Peter H. Campan, (not "Campo", as his name appears in the *Times* official list of July 29) Company D, Seventh Michigan, was mortally wounded at Boonsboro. When his captain called to see him at the hospital, and told him that he was badly wounded, Campan, who was only a boy, said, "Yes, Captain, I know I must die; but Captain," he concluded earnestly, *"have I always done my duty?"* Such are representative Michigan soldiers.

These regiments participated in most of the battles under Gen. Kilpatrick, during the fifteen days' cavalry fighting in Maryland and Pennsylvania and I therefore annex the substance of the official reports of the commanders of these regiments.

THE FIRST MICHIGAN CAVALRY

Headquarters Cavalry,
Second Brigade, Third Division Cavalry Corps

Capt. Jacob S. Green, Adjutant-General Third Division Cavalry Corps:
Sir—In compliance with the terms of the circular issued from Division

Headquarters on the 2d inst., I have the honor to report the First Michigan cavalry, as engaged under my command, in the following mentioned battles and skirmishes, since the 29th day of June last, as follows:

At Hanover, Pa., June 30, the regiment was not actively employed. It was ordered to support battery M, Second artillery, which was in position on a hill in rear of the town, until a late hour of the afternoon, when the battery was ordered to a new position. The regiment was ordered to hold the hill (the old position) by order of General Farnsworth, since deceased.

At the battle of Hunterstown, July 2, the regiment was put in line of battle on the right of the road, near the village. One squadron, under the command of Capt. A. W. Duggan, was detached to hold a road leading into the town from the rear. This platoon was actively engaged, and did good service.

On the 3d July, the regiment, with the others composing the Second brigade, was ordered to repel an attack on Gen. Meade's right. The position of the regiment was frequently changed during the day, but without meeting the enemy until about 4 P.M., when the Seventh Michigan cavalry, which had made a charge, and the Fifth Michigan cavalry, which had been deployed as skirmishers, were rapidly driven in by the enemy's cavalry (Hampton's brigade), the duty was devolved upon the First Michigan of saving battery M and the day, which was then going against us. Nobly did the "old First" do its duty. Charging in close column, the troopers using the sabre only, the host of rebel myrimonds were immediately swept from field. Never before in the history of this war has one regiment of National cavalry met an entire brigade of Confederate cavalry, (composed as this brigade was of regiments, each of which equalled in point of numbers the First Michigan) in open field—in a charge and defeated them. By the blessing of God, were not only defeated, but they were driven from the field in great confusion, and this regiment held the ground until ordered to a new position. I cannot say too much in praise of the officers and men of my command upon this occasion. That each did his duty is verified by the fact that the loss of the regiment in ten minutes was six officers and eighty men. Space in this report will forbid any mentioning individual deeds of heroism, but I shall embrace the opportunity offered by the Commanding General, in other form of doing so.

The division to which this regiment is attached moved early on the morning of the 4th ultimo to Emmitsburgh. From thence it proceeded toward Monterey. Before reaching that place the enemy was discovered in force upon the hills to the right of Fountaindale, a small village, some miles this side of Monterey—this regiment being in advance of the column—was sent upon a road leading from the right of the town and to Fairfield Gap. Upon reaching the gap, the enemy were found occupying it. A charge was made by Lieut.-Col. Stagg with one squadron which, with the aid of the other portion of the regiment, deployed as skirmishers, was successful in driving the enemy from the gap. The regiment held the position until the entire column and train had passed, though the enemy made a strong effort, with superior numbers, to drive it out. My command sustained a heavy loss here. Lieut.-Col. Stagg, leading the charge, had his horse killed under him, and falling, was seriously injured. Capt. Wm. R. Elliott, while bravely leading his company, was mortally wounded and died the next morning. Lieut. James S. McIlhenny, at that time, commanding Company G, was killed instantly at Capt. Elliott's side; 17 men also were lost in this engagement. I must embrace the present opportunity of paying a parting tribute to the memory of the noble men whose names I have above mentioned. Elliott and McIlhenny were, indeed, true types of the Union soldier. Both of them had volunteered, impressed with the idea of the justness of the cause of the Union. They devoted their whole time to their duties— ever ready and faithful in their discharge. They died as the Union soldier loves to die, leading in the charge. They died, too, earnestly endeavoring to perpetuate the beloved institutions of our country on the anniversary day of its birth. Two officers and six men were lost the same evening at Monterey.

On the 5th ultimo, at Smithfield, the regiment supported Battery M, United States Artillery, but sustained no loss. At Hagerstown on the 6th, it performed the same duty, and was equally fortunate in not meeting with loss.

At Boonsboro on the 8th, though the regiment was frequently under fire, it sustained no loss.

On the 12th, the regiment had the advance to Hagerstown. Five companies were deployed as skirmishers before the town. A squadron was ordered by Gen. Kilpatrick to charge into and through the town. The order was promptly executed, the enemy being driven in confusion from the streets, with the loss of several prisoners. One many only of this regiment was injured upon this day. On the 13th, the regiment was ordered on outpost duty, and was engaged with the enemy most of the day—sustaining a loss of three men severely wounded.

On the 14th this regiment was first to come to the relief of the Sixth Michigan cavalry, which had engaged the enemy near Falling Waters. The brave Weber had just made his gallant charge, as the regiment came up, joining with the Sixth, fighting on foot. The enemy were soon driven from the field. It was here that the Michigan brigade, led by the General commanding in person, did noble work. Each regiment vied with the other in deeds of daring. Five hundred prisoners, one gun, two caissons, three battle-flags, and a large quantity of small arms, attest the labor done. The First Michigan had the honor of capturing two of the three battle-flags, and the Forty-Seventh regiment Virginia infantry as well—at least so much as was on the field—being fifty-six men and five officers.

This engagement was the last that the regiment participated in under my command. Since that time Maj. Weber has had command of it. Permit me here to speak of the late Capt. Charles J. Snyder, of my regiment, who was mortally wounded while gallantly leading a squadron of the Eighteenth Pennsylvania cavalry, in the streets of Hagerstown, on the 6th July. He had been detailed from the regiment for some days as an Aide for Gen. Kilpatrick, and was ordered by that officer to assist in the charge. Fearlessly he went upon his duty, and, as an eyewitness informed me, nobly did he discharge it. Meeting six sturdy Confederates, he engaged them single handed, cutting three of them out of the saddle and putting the rest to flight, though he received the pistol shot which caused his death, and a saber cut on the head as well, early in the melee. The memory of this brave and noblehearted man will ever be cherished with brotherly fondness by officers and men of the First Michigan cavalry.

Very respectfully,

C. H. Town, Col. Com'g.

Maj. Brewer, who now commands the regiment, reports it to have been engaged on the 24th July for several hours in the attack on Hill's column at Newby's Cross-roads, where seven men were lost. On the 29th ult. the regiment, under Maj. Brewer, made a reconnaissance to Salem and Barber's Cross-roads, having slight skirmishes at both places, capturing a number of prisoners, and destroying a saw-mill and other buildings belonging to Maj. Williams, who is attached to Mosby's guerrilla band.

INCIDENTS

It was Sergts. Alphonso Chilson and James R. Lyon, of the First Michigan, who captured the Forty-seventh Virginia colors, together with a Major and seventy men at Falling Waters. The Forty-seventh was deployed, the Major and forty men were standing together in a hollow, when Sergt. Chilson marched up to the flag-bearer and seized the flag, at the same time Sergt. Lyon ordered the whole party to surrender, which order was very quickly obeyed, the rebels throwing down their arms. Passing them to the rear, Sergts. Chilson and Lyon captured twenty more men of the same regiment, all of whom they safely escorted to the rear. Privates Edward Ives and Edward Clark, in the same battle, captured the colors of the Fortieth Virginia regiment near the pontoon bridge, and while the rebels were destroying the bridge.

Capt. Snyder, who was in the first attack upon Hagerstown, was shot on Potomac Street, the ball entering on the left side of the abdomen, and coming out near the opposite without injuring the intestines. He was engaged with the enemy some twenty minutes and drove them three hundred yards after receiving his wounds, and feeling weak he then dismounted in front of the Franklin Hotel, where he was taken in and kindly cared for by the proprietor, and the citizens generally. A few minutes after this our troops were driven from the town, and not until a week afterward, when the town was taken possession of by Gen. Kilpatrick, was the fate of Capt. Snyder and others known. As our advance guard marched in Capt. Snyder was seen on the hotel balcony. He was doing well at that time, and when the troops moved forward all his most intimate friends bid him good-bye, and congratulated him upon having a "six weeks' leave of absence wound." He was in good spirits and spoke hopefully of joining the command soon. After leaving him thus, the shock the announcement of his death one week afterward gave his friends can well be imagined. He died of lockjaw.

THE FIGHT ON THE MOUNTAIN

At Fairfield Gap, one squadron, under Capt. Wells, deployed as skirmishers, while the second squadron, Capt. Elliott, of Company C, killed and Lieut. McIlhenny, of Company G, killed, charged. The horse of Lieut.-Col. Stagg, who led the charge, was shot, and falling upon him the Colonel received severe internal injuries. Surgeon Wooster sent him to Washington, but Col. Stagg's spirits would not permit him to remain there, and accordingly he rejoined the regiment at Berlin. Remaining one night he was again compelled to leave on account of his injuries. The regiment held the Gap for three hours. Company C lost 20 men. One squadron, under Capt. Brevoort and Adjutant Mathews, was in advance of the main column going over the mountain and received the first charge of grape and canister fired by the enemy that dark, stormy night. Capt. Brevoort, with commendable foresight, just before the cannon was fired, placed his men on either side of the road, thereby saving many lives, for when the enemy fired, they aimed their piece as near as they could in the dark at the head of the column. Not a man in the extreme front was injured, while there were several severely injured a little further to the rear.

A Narrow Escape

At the fight at Williamsport, when our line was compelled to fall back hastily, a party of eight men, composed of Lieut. Calerick, Sergt.-Major DeWitt C. Smith, Chief Bugler Rice, of the First Michigan and one man from the Fifth New York, two from the First [West] Virginia, and two from the Sixth Michigan, who had been with the advanced line of skirmishers, found themselves suddenly cut off, and enveloped within the enemy's line of skirmishers. Just as they had got into a barn-yard, surrounded by a high fence, to escape notice, two or three of the enemy espied them, but as it was nearly dark, they were not recognized—particularly after one of them answered the others that "these are our fellows." Abandoning their horses, the party sallied forth during the night to escape. Running upon the enemy's pickets at every point, they fell back, and awaited daylight. All the next day the rebels were in sight, and the party remained concealed by a fence between the two wheat fields. At night they made another unsuccessful attempt to get out of the lines, and finally fell in with some citizens, who furnished them citizens' clothing, and with whom, thus disguised, they remained for nearly a week, until, in fact, our troops again advanced upon Williamsport—the day the rebels recrossed the Potomac. Another party of eight skirmishers, under Sergt. Waterman, was cut off in the same fight. They escaped by taking a round-about route, passing through Louden, Chambersburgh, and Monterey to Hagerstown, where they rejoined their command. In the fight at Gettysburgh Capts. Alexander and Haskell and Lieut. Hickey escaped.

FIFTH MICHIGAN CAVALRY—MAJOR DRAKE

June 30—Moved from Littlestown, Penn., toward Hanover, Penn.; met the enemy; four squadrons dismounted as skirmishers, the remaining four squadrons in reserve, mounted; drove the enemy after severe skirmishing, from the field, and at night bivouacked in Hanover.

July 1—Marched from Hanover to Berlin, Penn.

July 2—Marched for Gettysburgh; arrived there on the morning of the 3d. The regiment was rear guard.

July 3—At 10 A.M. moved out and met the enemy on the right at Gettysburgh. The regiment was dismounted to fight on foot. On the left of the brigade Major Ferry was killed. Participated in several charges that day.

July 4—Moved from Gettysburgh toward Emmettsbur; Co. A was dismounted to skirmish on the line of march. Proceeded to Monterey, Md., in the mountains. Seven squadrons dismounted to fight—two squadrons remained mounted and charged toward the rebel battery. Three of the seven squadrons moved to the right of the main road, three miles from Emmettsburgh and dismounted; captured a train and prisoners, the whole command participating.

July 5—Proceeded to Smithsburgh, burning train on the way; two squadrons dismounted. Moved out at night, the regiment serving as rear guard.

July 6—Arrived at Boonsboro; moved to Hagerstown and dismounted. Remained in rear, as support or reserve. Proceeded toward Williamsport, Md., the regiment was dismounted and supported the battery by the road. Mounted and moved toward Boonsboro, bivouacking at Jones' Cross Roads.

July 7—Arrived at Boonsboro, remained during the day and night.

July 8—Moved out on the pike toward Funkstown; deployed as skirmishers on the right, on foot. Col. Alger was wounded here. Charged and drove the enemy in force from a wood, which was afterward hotly shelled. Subsequently, the enemy fell rapidly back, while the regiment pursued him closely until dark. Returned to Boonsboro at night.

July 9—Remained quielty at Boonsboro during day and night.

July 10—Proceeded to the right of Funkstown and picketed the right during day and night.

July 11—Still on picket and support for the battery.

July 12—Moved toward Hagerstown. Charged through the city, everywhere driving the enemy. Lieut.-Col. Gould was wounded in the charge. Two squadrons dismounted on the left of the city and drove a superior force from its position. Picketed during the rest of the day and night.

July 13—The regiment remained on picket in and around the city for the day and night.

July 14—Moved out of Hagerstown in the advance to Williamsport; charged into the town. Met no considerable force. Moved to the right of the town and up the river bank and drove a small force of the enemy's rear guard across the river. Captured a considerable number of prisoners. Rejoined the brigade at Falling Waters.

July 15—Marched to Boonsboro.

July 16—Marched to Berlin, on the Potomac, and remained day and night.

July 17—Crossed to Purcelville and Snicker's Gap, arriving at the latter place about A.M. Dismounted and employed as skirmishers. After skirmishing some time, took possession of, and held the Gap for the night. Several prisoners were captured.

July 18—Remained in possession of the Gap all day, and then returned to Purcelville.

July 19—Marched from Purcelville to Upperville.

July 20—Moved toward Ashby's Gap; dismounted, deployed as skirmishers, and moved up into the mountains; the advance resisting a cavalry charge, while the skirmishers, driving the enemy from the Gap, took possession of it. Returned to Upperville same night.

July 21—Still at Upperville. On 22d moved to Manassas Railroad.

July 23—Moved to Amissville.

July 24—Moved to Newby's Crossroads in advance, ten squadrons dismounting to fight; deployed as skirmishers and moved on the right. Two squadrons, mounted, remained in line in front. After some skirmishing, obeyed order to fall back.

C. P. Drake

Major, Fifth Michigan Com'g.

Sixth Michigan Cavalry, Col. Gray

On the morning of June 30, this regiment, with the Fifth, occupied Littlestown, Penn., where Company A was out on a reconnaissance toward Westminster; the remainder of the regiment (nine companies) proceeded to Hanover. On approaching the last named place, we came upon the enemy's skirmishers, whom we drove to their guns, which we unexpectedly found posted on our right, supported by a large force of cavalry. Their battery opened upon us, when we withdrew. In making this movement, we were completely flanked by another body of the enemy's cavalry, outnumbering my command six to one. I placed to companies (B and F) in position to protect our rear and to check the enemy's advance. These companies met, by counter charges, three successive charges of the enemy, with a loss on our part from 15 to 20 captured, and a loss to the enemy of several wounded and captured. The regiment then moved by the left of the road to Hanover, and there reported to Gen. Custer.

Company A having been afterward called in from Westminster Road, joined a portion of the Fifth Michigan cavalry and, later in the day had an engagement with a cavalry force of the enemy.

On reporting to Gen. Custer at Hanover, this regiment was at once deployed as skirmishers, forming a line of battle one mile in length, advanced upon the enemy and drove them until they withdrew.

On the evening of July 2, the regiment encountered the enemy's cavalry at Hunterstown. Company A, under command of Capt. H. A. Thompson, charged a brigade of cavalry, and, though suffering great loss, so checked the enemy as to enable our battery to be placed in a position. Three other squadrons then dismounted, and, with their rifles, drove the enemy back, when the guns of our battery caused them to precipitately leave the field.

July 3, 1863—At Gettysburgh, the regiment was ordered to the support of the battery: four companies being pushed forward in front dismounted; four remaining, through a great part of the engagement, mounted and immediately on the left of the battery, exposed to the shot and shell of the enemy's guns. The other companies were engaged as skirmishers to the front and right.

July 4—At Monterey, when the attack was made on the enemy's train, this regiment dismounted and deployed as skirmishers, fought the enemy who were advantageously posted in the woods on either side of the road and supported by two guns. Here again the enemy was driven with great loss on their part and slight on ours.

July 5—At Smithburgh this regiment was employed in supporting the battery.

July 6—At Hagerstown, the regiment having been in rear of the column of march, was ordered to the front, but on arriving there, Gen. Custer, having driven the enemy, ordered us back.

Same day, at Williamsport, passing in the direct range of the enemy's guns, thereby losing one officer killed and three men wounded, the regiment was posted on the front and to the right of our battery, and connecting with the skirmishers of the First Michigan cavalry, protected our own guns and held the enemy, who was advancing on our right until the remainder of the command left the position—the First and Sixth being the last to retire.

July 8—At Boonsboro, this regiment was deployed to the left of the Hagerstown road, and after a sharp and hotly contested engagement, lasting several hours, repulsed and routed the enemy, and drove him three miles, and until night closed the pursuit. The rebel Gen. Stuart was, in person, directing the assault in front of this regiment on that occasion.

July 11—This regiment was ordered to do picket duty before Hagerstown—its line extending from the Cavetown and Hagerstown turnpike on the right, toward Funkstown on the left. Here during the entire day we were engaged skirmishing with the enemy's sharpshooters. Our loss was only two wounded; the enemy was seen to carry some of his dead and wounded from his line.

July 12—Participated in the capture of Hagerstown.

July 14—At Falling Waters, this regiment being in advance of all others, came upon a division of the enemy's infantry in a very strong position behind earthworks on the crown of a hill. The advance guard, Companies B and F, under command of Major P. A. Weber, charged them up to and within their fortifications. An entire brigade surrendered to this mere handful of men, when another brigade, drawn up in line in rear of the first, opened a murderous fire upon the gallant little band, in which the others who had just surrendered also joined, and the survivors were compelled to withdraw, leaving the bodies of many of their gallant and lamented comrades within the rebel works, a witness of their noble and heroic daring. The remainder of the regiment deployed as skirmishers, then engaged the vastly superior force of the enemy, but overpowered by numbers, fell back to the cover of a hill, where they were joined by the First Michigan cavalry. These two regiments then marched forward, charged the enemy, who fled with great loss. The fight soon became a rout and soon nothing was to be seen of that division but the dead and wounded covering the fields and the crowds of prisoners in our hands.

July 20—This regiment participated in the capture of Ashby's Gap, and by order of Col. Town, brigade commander, proceeded rapidly to Berry's Ford, on the Shenandoah, where we encountered the enemy strongly entrenched on the opposite side of the river. After a skirmish, lasting some hours, there being no means of crossing the river, we were ordered to return. Our loss was three wounded.

July 24—Engaged in the reconnaissance from Amissville to Newby's Cross Roads. This regiment, under command of Lieut.-Col. Foote, was deployed as skirmishers, and occupied the left of the line. After driving the enemy's line of skirmishers and accomplishing the object of the reconnaissance, the command was ordered back to Amissville. On the return, this regiment, occupying the (then) right, and in a narrow lane, found itself flanked by a brigade of the enemy's infantry, but succeeded in effecting the movement with but little loss.

Geo. Gray, Colonel
Commanding Sixth Michigan cavalry

Seventh Michigan Cavalry — Col. Mann.

At Hanover, Pa., on the 30th of June, the regiment having the advance of the brigade in its rapid return from Abbottstown, was thrown into position on the left of the turnpike, to the left and front of battery M, Second United States artillery. Two squadrons were dismounted and advanced as skirmishers, under the command of Lieut.-Col. Litchfield. In the progress of the action the regiment was moved to the right of the town as support to battery M. The skirmishes, after having advanced beyond the town and exhausted their ammunition, was withdrawn. At about 5 o'clock P.M. Companies C, H and E, under command of Maj. Newcombe, were sent to occupy the town, which they took possession of and held until night when the enemy withdrew.

At Hagerstown, on the 2d of July, the regiment, except one squadron held in reserve, was advanced on the left as dismounted skirmishers.

At Gettysburgh, on the 3d of July, on the extended right of our line during the early part of the day, the regiment, as reserve and as a support to battery M, occupied various positions on the field. At about 4 o'clock P.M., the regiment was ordered to charge the advancing line of the enemy's skirmishers, who were closely supported by their cavalry reserve.

A desperate but unequal, hand-to-hand conflict here occurred. The regiment being finally obliged to retire twice, rallied under a sharp fire from the enemy, without support or cover, and returned to the charge, and held the field until the advance of the First Michigan.

At Monterey on the night of the 4th of July, two companies, under command of Capt. Armstrong, were detached to hold the mountain road on the right. The remainder of the regiment fought on the right as dismounted skirmishers.

At Smithburgh July 5, the regiment supported battery M, and occupied the extreme left.

At Hagerstown July 6, the regiment having supported the battery in the early part of the affair, was afterward advanced on the right nearly past the town, when it was dismounted and thrown forward as skirmishers, driving the enemy beyond the town, and was then recalled. At Williamsport same day, supported a battery.

July 8, at Boonsboro, in the early part of the action, supported battery M, on the right of the Hagerstown road. As our line of skirmishers were falling back, Maj. Newcombe, with his battalion, dismounted and advanced to their support. The line advanced under a heavy fire and drove the enemy from the woods. Reinforcements coming up a charge was made, and the enemy were driven from the field. The remainder of the regiment supported the skirmishers, and were exposed to a heavy fire.

On the 12th of July, the regiment being temporarily attached to the First Brigade, with it entered Hagerstown under a sharp fire from the enemy. In the afternoon the regiment was advanced to support the infantry at the extreme right of the town.

At Falling Waters, July 14, on coming into action, Maj. Granger was dispatched to the right, where, from the enemy a 10-pound Parrott gun which, after having been turned against the enemy with great effect, he brought from the field. Another portion of the regiment went to the support of the skirmishers, and the remainder as a support to Battery M. The enemy's column advancing to charge this battery, that portion of the right supporting it—seventy sabres—advanced to the charge and brought from the field 400 prisoners, with the battle-flag of the Fifty-fifth Virginia. The dismounted skirmishers of this regiment captured the Colonel of the Fifty-fifth Virginia, with several other officers and a squad of men.

Geo. K. Newcombe

Major Seventh Michigan Cavalry, Com'g.

MOSBY AND THE SUTLERS

Mosby and his command of bushwhackers have had rich pickings lately among the sutler's trains. When the Union army had passed on toward the Rappahannock, on its return trip from Maryland and Pennsylvania, the usual swarm of sutlers—most of whom owing to the position of the army—followed on from Alexandria and Washington. Their trains contained from 15 to 50 wagons each, and generally without any other guard than the sutlers and employees. Some of these trains have reached the army without interruption, but a majority have been pounced upon by the loquacious Mosby, who carries away all he can of the useful and destroys the remainder of their loads. Mosby uses a great deal of strategy in the capture of trains. He has a particular penchant for sutler's goods because he generally runs less risk in attacking them, because not so well guarded, and then Government trains only carry the coarser commodities. Recently he rode half a day with a sutler's train, between Alexandria and Fairfax Court-house, making himself quite familiar with the business of his traveling companions, and representing himself to be a Quartermaster in some cavalry regiment. When arrived near Fairfax Court-house the train halted. The quondam Quartermaster tied his horse to a wagon and moved off for the alleged purpose of taking a nap. He soon returned, however, with his party, and captured the whole train. Unfortunately for Mosby, but fortunate for the sutlers, one of our cavalry squads soon after started in pursuit, and recaptured all but two or three of the forty or more wagons originally taken.

But Mosby's career will soon be brought to a close, if the recent order, which compels all citizens residing in that portion of Virginia—east of the Blue Ridge and north of the Rappahannock—to take the oath of allegiance or go outside of our lines, is vigorously enforced. Mosby professes to have only sixty men, but then he has the white population of the district he roams as auxiliaries, to picket towns, roads, act as spies, &c. Remove these agents, and Mosby would soon be forced to seek another field to operate in.

How a Surgeon's Ambulance Was Saved

When, on the 30th of June, 1863, the rear of Gen. Kilpatrick's cavalry division was attacked in the town of Hanover, Penn., the first charge fell upon a remnant of the Eighteenth Pennsylvania cavalry. This command was somewhat scattered, and the rebels, passing through it, came upon the private ambulance of Dr. Wood, chief surgeon of the division. Two soldiers, named Spaulding and Forsyth, occupied this vehicle—both hospital attendants. As the enemy approached, they made a vigorous attack upon the covering of the wagon with their swords—cutting a dozen or more holes in the top—when Spaulding, who was sick, suggested to Forsyth, who was driving, that he (Spaulding) should drive, and the other drive off the assailants with a six-shooter one of the party had. This arrangement was carried into effect; the enemy were driven away, and the worthy surgeon's traps were saved to the service.

A Brave Soldier

In the same battle, Folger, a private in Company H, Fifth New York cavalry, performed an act of great coolness and daring. He got mixed up some way in the charge upon the Eighteenth Pennsylvania cavalry, not having time to reload his carbine, he picked up a loaded one some person had dropped, shot a horse upon which the rebel Col. Payne was riding, the falling into a tan-vat, and it was with difficulty Folger saved him from drowning. Just at the moment the Colonel was safely out of the vat, his orderly rode up, and presenting a pistol to Folger, ordered him to surrender. Folger hesitated, but looking up the street and seeing the advance of the Fifth in the celebrated charge made at that time, suddenly seized upon his unloaded carbine, and aiming it at Mr. Orderly, in no very complimentary terms, ordered him to surrender or he would blow his brains out. The orderly, completely taken by surprise at this turn of affairs, surrendered without making any resistance, so that young Folger, youthful though he be, by the display of a little coolness and daring in extremes, not only saved himself from capture, but captured a colonel and a private from the ranks of the enemy during the heat of battle.

Appendix B
Gen. George A. Custer's "Lost" Report of the Battle on the East Cavalry Field, Gettysburg, July 3, 1863

For reasons that are a mystery, Brig. Gen. George A. Custer's complete report of the Michigan Cavalry Brigade's role in the fighting on the East Cavalry Field does not appear in the Official Records of the Civil War. Instead, a report that is largely an itinerary of the 6th and 7th Michigan Cavalry and of Pennington's Battery appears, but the material provides little insight into Custer's thoughts regarding the epic clash on the East Cavalry Field.

In his speech dedicating the Michigan Cavalry Brigade monument, Kidd quoted extensively from this report, but efforts to locate its full text have been both fruitless and extensive. I spent a number of months trying to locate the original in the National Archives and other repositories, and I also consulted with a number of prominent Custer scholars to determine whether they might know its whereabouts.

Those efforts were, I am sorry to report, frustrating. All I managed to locate was a significant portion of the missing report, which was included in a very early comprehensive biography of Custer, Frederick Whittaker's two-volume A Complete Life of General George A. Custer, *published in 1876, just a few months after the Little Big Horn tragedy. The fragment is very useful to understanding Custer's strategy and tactics for the fight on the East Cavalry Field, but it would also be a major contribution to enhancing our understanding of the fight at Hanover on June 30 and the engagement at Hunterstown on July 2. Alas, this insight may well be lost to history for good, which is truly a shame.*

While I would prefer to present the entire report, it does not appear possible. Because the remaining fragment has been ignored by nearly all modern accounts of the epic fight on the East Cavalry Field, I present that fragment that appeared in Whittaker's biography here in the hope that it sheds some light on Custer's thoughts and strategy for this epic encounter. In order to assist the reader in making better sense of this report, I have added several interpretive notes in the text, which typically appear in brackets.

At an early hour on the morning of the 3d, I received an order, through a staff-officer of the Brigadier-General commanding [Brig. Gen. Judson Kilpatrick, commander of the Third Division of the Army of the Potomac's Cavalry Corps] the division, to move at once my command, and follow the First brigade on the road leading from Two Taverns to Gettysburg. Agreeably to the above instructions, my column was formed and moved out on the road designated, when a staff officer of Brigadier General [David M.] Gregg, commanding Second division, ordered me to take my command and place it in position on the pike leading from York to Gettysburg, which position formed the extreme right of our battle on that day. Upon arriving at the point designated, I immediately placed my command in position, facing toward Gettysburg. At the same time I caused reconnaissances to be made on my front, right, and rear, but failed to discover any considerable force of the enemy. Everything remained quiet till 10 A.M., when the enemy appeared on my right flank and opened upon me with a battery of six guns. Leaving two guns and a regiment to hold my first position and cover the road leading to Gettysburg [the Hanover Road], I shifted the remaining portion of my command, forming a new line of battle at right angles to my former line. The enemy had obtained correct range of my new position, and were pouring solid shot and shell into my command with great accuracy. Placing two sections of Battery M, Second (regular) Artillery [also known as Pennington's battery], in position, I ordered them to silence the enemy's battery, which order, notwithstanding the superiority of the enemy's position, was successfully accomplished in a very short space of time. My line, as it then existed, was shaped like the letter L, the shorter branch formed of the section of Battery [M], Second Artillery, supported by a portion of the Sixth Michigan cavalry on the right, while the Seventh Michigan cavalry, still further to the right and in advance, was held in readiness to repel any attack the enemy might make, coming on the Oxford road. The Fifth Michigan cavalry was dismounted, and ordered to take position in front of my centre and left. The First Michigan cavalry was held in column of squadrons to observe the movements of the enemy. I ordered fifty men to be sent one mile and a half on the Oxford road, while a detachment of equal size was sent one mile and a half on the road leading from Gettysburg to York, both detachments being under the command of the gallant Major Webber, who from time to time kept me so well informed of the movements of the enemy that I was enabled to make my dispositions with complete success. At 12 o'clock, an order was transmitted to me from the Brigadier-General commanding the division, by one of his aides, directing me, upon being relieved by a brigade of the Second Division, to move with my command and form a junction with the First brigade on the extreme left. On the arrival of the brigade of the Second Division, commanded by Colonel [John B.] McIntosh [of the 3d Pennsylvania Cavalry], I prepared to execute the order. Before I had left my position, Brigadier-General Gregg, commanding the Second Division, arrived with his entire command. Learning the true condition of affairs on my front, and rightly conjecturing that the enemy was making his dispositions for attacking our position, Brigadier-General Gregg ordered me to remain in the position I then occupied.

The enemy was soon after reported to be advancing on my front. The detachment of fifty men sent on the Oxford road were driven in, and at the same time the enemy's line of skirmishers, consisting of dismounted cavalry, appeared on the crest of the ridge of hills on my front. The line extended beyond my left. To repel their advance, I ordered the Fifth cavalry to a more advanced position, with instructions to maintain their ground at all hazards. Colonel Alger, commanding the Fifth, assisted by Majors Trowbridge and Ferry, of the same regiment, made such admirable disposition of their men behind fences and other defenses, as enabled them to successfully repel the repeated advances of a greatly superior force. I attributed their success in great measure to the fact that this regiment is armed with the Spencer repeating rifle, which, in the hands of brave, determined men, like those composing the Fifth Michigan cavalry, is in my estimation, the most effective fire-arm that our cavalry can adopt. Colonel Alger held his ground until his men had exhausted their ammunition, when he was compelled to fall back on the main body. The beginning of this movement was the signal for the enemy to charge, which they did with two regiments, mounted and dismounted. I at once ordered the Seventh Michigan cavalry, Colonel Mann, to charge the advancing column of the enemy. The ground over which we had to pass was very unfavorable for the maneuvering of cavalry, but despite all obstacles this regiment advanced boldly to the assault, which was executed in splendid style, the enemy being driven from field to field, until our advance reached a high and unbroken fence, behind which the enemy were strongly posted. Nothing daunted, Colonel Mann, followed by the main body of his regiment, bravely rode up to the fence and discharged their revolvers in the very face of the foe. No troops could have maintained this position; the Seventh was, therefore, compelled to retire, followed by twice the number of the enemy.

By this time Colonel Alger of the Fifth Michigan cavalry had succeeded in mounting a considerable portion of his regiment, and gallantly advanced to the assistance of the Seventh, whose further pursuit by the enemy he checked. At the same time an entire brigade of the enemy's cavalry, consisting of four regiments, appeared just over the crest in our front. They were formed in columns of regiments. To meet this overwhelming force I had but one available regiment, the First Michigan cavalry, and the fire of Battery M, Second Regular Artillery. I at once ordered the First to charge, but learned at the same moment that similar orders had been given by Brigadier-General Gregg. As before stated, the First was formed in column of battalions. Upon receiving the order to charge, Colonel Town, placing himself at the head of his command, ordered the "trot" and sabres to be drawn. In this manner this gallant body of men advanced to the attack of a force outnumbering them five to one. In addition to this numerical superiority the enemy had the advantage of position, and were exultant over the repulse of the Seventh Michigan cavalry. All these facts considered would seem to render success on the part of the First impossible. No so, however. Arriving within a few yards of the enemy's column, the charge was ordered, and with a yell that spread terror before them, the First Michigan cavalry, led by Colonel Town, rode upon the front rank of the enemy, and sabring all who came within reach. For a moment, but only a moment, that long, heavy column stood its ground; then, unable to withstand the impetuosity of our attack, it gave way in a disorderly rout, leaving cast numbers of dead and wounded in our possession, while the First, being masters of the field, had the proud satisfaction of seeing the much-vaunted chivalry, led by their favorite commander, seek safety in headlong flight. I cannot find language to express my high appreciation of the gallantry and daring displayed by the officers and men of the First Michigan cavalry. They advanced to the charge of a vastly superior force with as much order and precision as if going upon parade; and I challenge the annals of warfare to produce a more brilliant or successful charge of cavalry than the one just recounted. Nor must I forget to acknowledge the invaluable assistance rendered by Battery M, Second Regiment of Artillery, in this charge. Our success in driving the enemy from the field, is due, in a great measure, to the highly efficient manner in which the battery was handled by Lieutenant A. C. M. Pennington, assisted by Lieutenants Clark, Woodruff, and Hamilton. The enemy made but slight demonstrations against us during the remainder of the day, except in one instance he attempted to turn my left flank, which attempt was most gallantly met and successfully frustrated by Second Lieutenant J. H. Kellogg, with Company H Sixth Michigan cavalry. We held possession of the field until dark, during which time we collected our dead and wounded. At dark I returned with my command to Two Taverns, where I encamped for the night.

In this engagement my command lost in killed, wounded and missing, a total of five hundred and forty-two. Among the killed I regret to record the name of Major N. H. Ferry of the Fifth Michigan cavalry, who fell while heroically cheering on his men. It would be impossible for me to particularize those instances deserving especial mention; all, both men and officers, did their duty. There were many cases of personal heroism, but a list of their names would make my report too extended. To Colonel Town, commanding the First Michigan cavalry, and to the officers and men of his regiment, for the gallant manner in which they drove the enemy from the field, great praise is due.

Colonel Mann of the Seventh Michigan cavalry, and Colonel Alger, of the Fifth Michigan cavalry, as well as the officers of their commands, are entitled to much credit for their united efforts in repelling the advance of the enemy. The Sixth Michigan cavalry rendered good service by guarding both my right and left flank; also by supporting Battery M, under a very hot fire from the enemy's battery. Colonel Gray, commanding the regiment, was constantly seen wherever his presence was most needed, and is deserving of special mention. I desire to commend to your favorable notice Lieutenants Pennington, Clark, Woodruff, and Hamilton of Battery M, Second Artillery, for the zeal and ability displayed by each on this occasion. My thanks are personally due to the following named members of my staff, who on many occasions exhibited remarkable gallantry in transmitting and executing my orders on the field: Captain A. G. Drew, Sixth Michigan cavalry, Assistant Inspector General, First Lieutenant R. Baylis, Fifth Michigan cavalry, Acting Assistant Adjutant-General, First Lieutenant William H. Wheeler, First Michigan cavalry, A.D.C. First Lieutenant William Colerick, First Michigan cavalry, A.D.C. I desire also to mention two of my buglers,

Joseph Fought, company D, Fifth U.S. Cavalry, and Peter Boehn, company B, Fifth U.S. Cavalry; also Orderlies Norval Churchill, company L, First Michigan cavalry, George L. Foster, company C, First Michigan cavalry, and Benjamin H. Butler, company M, First Michigan cavalry.

Respectfully submitted,

G. A. Custer

Brigadier-General Commanding Second Brigade

Jacob L. Greene,

Assistant Adjutant-General

Bibliographic Essay

This volume is intended to be a companion to my other volume of Kidd's work, *One of Custer's Wolverines: The Civil War Letters of Bvt. James Harvey Kidd, Sixth Michigan Cavalry* (Kent, Ohio: Kent State University Press, 2000). That volume contains a full, detailed bibliography that includes all of the sources consulted in preparing that volume. Many, if not most, of those same sources were also consulted in the preparation of this book. The works referenced in this bibliographic essay represent a good cross-section of some of the more valuable references, and I hope that this essay provides some guidance to those interested in learning more about the many issues discussed by Kidd in his writings.

Any study of Kidd's career must begin with Kidd's classic memoir, *Personal Recollections of a Cavalryman in Custer's Michigan Brigade* (Ionia, Mich.: Sentinel Printing Co., 1908). As perhaps the Civil War's finest single brigade of cavalry, the proud members of the Michigan Cavalry Brigade left behind a rich written record. Useful sources include the prolific Lt. Samuel Harris's *Michigan Brigade of Cavalry at the Battle of Gettysburg, July 3, 1863, Under Command of Brig.-Gen. Geo. A. Custer* (Cass City, Mich.: Privately printed, 1894); Asa B. Isham's regimental history, *An Historical Sketch of the Seventh Regiment Michigan Volunteer Cavalry from Its Organization, in 1862, to Its Muster-Out, in 1865* (New York: Town Topics Publishing Co., 1893); William O. Lee's compilation, *Personal and Historical Sketches and Facial History of and by Members of the Seventh Michigan Volunteer Cavalry, 1862–1865.* (Detroit: Ralston-Stroup Printing Co., 1904); Lt. Robert C. Wallace's

A Few Memories of a Long Life (Fairfield, Wash.: Ye Galleon Press, 1988); and John Robertson's *Michigan in the War* (Lansing, Mich.: W. S. George & Co., 1882).

Of course, no study of the American Civil War is complete without consulting *The War of the Rebellion: A Compilation of the Official Records of the Union and Confederate Armies*, 128 vols. (Washington, D.C.: GPO, 1880–1901) and the *Supplement to the Official Records of the Union and Confederate Armies* 100 vols. (Wilmington, N.C.: Broadfoot Publishing Co., 1990).

Essential secondary sources are Gregory J. W. Urwin's *Custer Victorious: The Civil War Battles of General George Armstrong Custer* (Rutherford, N.J.: Associated University Presses, 1983) and Edward G. Longacre's *Custer and His Wolverines: The Michigan Cavalry Brigade 1861–1865* (Conshohocken, Pa.: Combined Books, 1997). No study of Civil War cavalry is complete without reliance upon Stephen Z. Starr's monumental three-volume history of the Federal mounted arm, *The Union Cavalry in the Civil War* (Baton Rouge: Louisiana State University, 1979–84). For insight into the role of the cavalry in the Wilderness campaign, and to better understand the importance of this overlooked campaign, the best single volume written to date is Gordon C. Rhea's fine *The Battle of the Wilderness, May 5–6, 1864* (Baton Rouge: Louisiana State University Press, 1994). The only book-length study of cavalry operations in the Gettysburg campaign is Edward G. Longacre's *The Cavalry at Gettysburg* (Rutherford, N.J.: Fairleigh-Dickinson University Press, 1986). The best single-volume study of Sheridan's Shenandoah Valley campaign of 1864 is Jeffry D. Wert's *From Winchester to Cedar Creek: The Shenandoah Campaign of 1864* (Carlisle, Pa.: South Mountain Press, 1987), although Edward J. Stackpole's *Sheridan in the Shenandoah*, 2d ed. (Harrisburg, Pa. Stackpole Books, 1992) is also useful.

A significant portion of this book is devoted to the life and career of Bvt. Maj. Gen. George Armstrong Custer, the "Boy General with the Golden Locks." Few historical figures have generated more written words than George Custer and the disaster that befell him at the Little Big Horn on June 25, 1876. There is a mind-boggling volume of material available for study by the interested student. With the help of my friend Brian C. Pohanka, I was able to identify a few critical sources and focus my study of Custer and the men of the 7th Cavalry on a few important works. Those include, but are not limited to, what are probably the two finest biographies of Custer, Frederick Whitaker's *A Complete Life of General George A. Custer*, 2 vols. (New York: Sheldon, 1876) and Jeffry D. Wert's *Custer: The Controversial Life of*

George Armstrong Custer (New York: Simon and Schuster, 1996). Another particularly useful volume is Paul Andrew Hutton's anothology *The Custer Reader* (Lincoln: University of Nebraska Press, 1992), which contains a number of especially valuable essays by participants as well as by modern historians. Finally, John M. Carroll's many works are important, but perhaps none more so than his *Custer in the Civil War: His Unfinished Memoirs* (San Rafael, Calif.: Presidio Press, 1977).

Hundreds of books have been written about Custer's career as an Indian fighter. It would be impossible to read all of them, and I did not attempt to do so. Instead, I selected a few particularly useful works and focused on them. For background and insight into Custer's early career as an Indian fighter, I referred to Stan Hoig's *The Battle of the Washita* (New York: Doubleday, 1976), as well as several of the essays in Hutton's *The Custer Reader*. Among the works that I focused on in my crash course on the tragedy of the Little Big Horn include Edgar I. Stewart's classic *Custer's Luck* (Norman: University of Oklahoma Press, 1995), which, while a bit dated, remains one of the classic works on the campaigns of the summer of 1876. I also emphasized John S. Gray's *Centennial Campaign: The Sioux War of 1876* (Norman: University of Oklahoma Press, 1988). For details on the life and career of Capt. Myles W. Keogh, one of the troop commanders who followed Custer to his death at the Little Big Horn, no work is more important than the anthology edited by John P. Langellier, Kurt Hamilton Cox, and Brian C. Pohanka, *Myles Keogh: The Life and Legend of an "Irish Dragoon" in the Seventh Cavalry* (El Segundo, Ca.: Upton and Sons, 1998).

Index